THORNS IN MY NEST

OVERCOMING REJECTIONS, PAST HURTS, & WOUNDS OF THE SPIRIT IN THE DARKEST OF TIMES

BY:
KEY-BE OLADIPO

BE-KEY PUBLISHING

LIMERICK, PA

THORNS IN MY NEST

Cover Design: Vision by Keebee Oladipo. Design brought to life by Unlimited Graphics, 357 W. Main Street, Trappe, PA 610-489-3770

First Printing December 2002   **ISBN: 0-9726036-0-3**

Additional copies of this book are available by mail.
Send correspondence to:
Be-Key Publishing
P.O. Box 1005
Royersford, PA 19468

Printed in the U. S. A. by:
Morris Publishing
3212 East Highway 30
Kearney, NE 68847
1-800-650-7888

Oladipo, Keebee, 1963-
        Thorns In My Nest: Overcoming Rejections, Past Hurts and Wounds of the Spirit in the Darkest of Times/ Keebee Oladipo

    1. Spiritual life—Christianity

DEDICATION

This book is dedicated To the King of Glory, The Lord God Almighty!!! Known in the three persons of the trinity as The Father, The Son and The Holy Spirit. You are my Jehovah-Kadesh, "The God that sanctifies." You are the Greatest Eagle that I have ever known. You have given me so much strength to endure hardship as a good soldier. Why you love me the way you do, I don't understand. Your love is the greatest. I thank you for this spiritual seed that you fathered and birthed in me. Give me the wisdom and strength to raise this child (your ministry) that you've placed in my care until it is full grown. I know this is only the beginning. I look forward to the fruit that will come out of this one seed. Thank you for the ministry in me, that ministers to me. You are that ministry to me. Use me for your glory. Use whatever it takes to keep me humbly in your presence. I give you all the glory, honor and praise that is due your name. **You are the King of kings and the Lord of lords. You are the mighty God that I adore. You are the prince of peace that blessed Lamb. You are God, You are...**

I AM

I DO WORSHIP YOU!

Thorns In My Nest

Isaiah 45:7-12

I form the light, and create darkness: I make peace, and create evil: I the Lord do all these things. Drop down, ye heavens, from above, and let the skies pour down righteousness: let the earth open, and let them bring forth salvation, and let righteousness spring up together; I the Lord have created it. Woe unto him that striveth with his Maker! Let the potsherd strive with the potsherds of the earth. Shall the clay say to him that fashioneth it, what makest thou? Or thy work, He hath no hands? Woe unto him that saith unto his father, What begettest thou? Or to the woman, What hast thou brought forth? Thus saith the Lord, the Holy One of Israel, and his Maker, Ask me of things to come concerning my sons, and concerning the work of my hands command ye me. I have made the earth, and created man upon it: I, even my hands, have stretched out the heavens, and all their host have I commanded.

Words From A Mentor's Heart

By: Prophetess Vedar Nichols
(The Eagle Known as "Mom")

"MENTORSHIP"

1 Corinthians 3:6-7, "Some plant, some water; God gives the increase."

The planter is not greater than the one who waters; both are needed to make the process complete. The principle of increase cannot come into operation without these two principles in operation within a person's life. The mentor could either be the planter, or the one who waters. The mentor must be able to discern what role he or she is supposed to perform in the life of the protégé.

The course that lies before the mentor is the call of "apostolic parenting." Deep down the mentor is a father or a mother to that person. He or she must maintain the strength of discernment otherwise they will certainly lose their protégé. Premature release can inevitably be damaging for a lifetime, because it can set the person being mentored on the wrong course.

I consider myself to be a planter, and I believe as such, the planter has the most difficult job. The planter gets the protégé in the new-conception state – the state that is unidentifiable to the flesh. Only the spirit of man can know. You first have to help them understand what they are to become, as well as what God has put inside of them. They must be convinced of their own worth by identifying themselves with Christ. As the planter, one has to help the mentored to see their potential, perfect and successful in the eyes of God.

As a planter, I have the responsibility of plowing through hard, unbroken ground, which is often stony, and dry. I must first prepare the soil of the person's heart with water. This is done by the expression of love, empathizing and showing compassion for their pain. The soil is watered with my tears from the heart as I listen their story. The preparation of the soil ensures that planting can take place. The soil cannot resist the seeds to be planted.

The roots of the seeds that are planted, connects with the soil once the process of death takes place. Within this seed lies the potential to produce fruit. After the seed dies to itself, then that potential can become a reality. The potential breaks through the soil in the form of a tiny stem. In time, the fruit will be yielded.

The mentor stands by as a guardian over the seeds that have been planted in the life of the protégé. He or she has to make sure they are not devoured, keeping the process from continuing. When it is time for the one who waters to enter into the protégé's life that, which is planted is nourished. This prevents the life of the protégé from drying up before it can bring forth the intended harvest. Remember, God brings the increase; God brings the intended harvest.

God is a God of the past, present and future. Everything is complete in His eyes. He already sees that person, as they will be. The mentor simply helps take the person to the next level, helps to take the person through the process of becoming in this earth realm, what the person already is in the realm of the Spirit. The one who is to water that person is being prepared to take him or her to levels beyond the planting levels, so fruition can occur.

The mentor loves the one that he or she is guiding. Yet, sometimes the love is hard to grasp, because the mentor acts as the iron sharpener. Yet, in the pain and friction, there is always love and perseverance in love. The mentor knows there is only a set amount of time for the student to complete the class. There is no time for delicate handling when there is a destiny waiting to be fulfilled in the person's life. The time allotted for arrival at the destination is always in the forefront of the mentor's mind.

Possession of a servant's heart on the part of the protégé is a necessary element, as the protégé is ever in the position of reception. When the mentor sees an eager heart to learn and serve, it is far easier for the mentor, the planter, to give all that he or she has to that person. Like Elisha and Elijah, the protégé must come humbly with the intent to serve, as well as learn. The agenda is destiny fulfillment on both sides. The way to get to that place is through submission to leadership.

In many ways, mentorship can be compared to spiritual pregnancy. The mentor is like an expectant mother, carrying within - a developing child. The protégé is carried as an "unborn baby" in the "womb." The child within cannot choose the mother, and cannot choose the "womb" in which he or she is being carried. The child has no capacity to accept his or her parentage by rejecting the one carrying him or her to birth. Likewise there can be no realistic ability to like or dislike the "womb" if the person wants to come forth in the end.

At times, though, the protégé may not agree with or even like the person God has selected to carry them to term. This is human nature and human prerogative. Yet, the issue of like over dislike has no relevance because to rebel against the "womb" is sure and sudden death. The "son " or "daughter" cannot rebel, or the most important elements of gestation will be missed – the mantles of the anointing that lies within the "womb" of the mentor. And what's more – the rebellion is against God Himself and His will.

The mentor has the anointing to impart and release mantles for the life of the person entrusted to him or her. These anointings come at moments of transition to new levels and dimensions in the spirit realm, in ministry, and in life in general. This also occurs when the person's ministry focus is about to shift.

The mentor must never try to appear perfect. He or she will be in danger of hurting him or herself or the protégé. The mentor must see himself and relate to the protégé as a real person who strives daily to walk humbly before God, and man.

Those who are called to be mentors need to prepare themselves. There is a new call in the land for you to "father and mother." This is a Kingdom call. The Spirit of Elijah is returning to the earth in order to bring restoration of the families. God is restoring the fathers back to the children and the children back to the fathers. This generation is not going to experience this restoration without spiritual fathers and mothers (mentors).

To my daughter, who challenged me. And yet still knew what she wanted and was determined to get what was rightfully yours, **YOU ARE AN EAGLE!** *You knew from the beginning you were never satisfied with the "chicken coop experience." You always knew you were born to soar!*

I love you... Soar with everything that is in you...

Mom

From the Heart of a Protégé

You taught me life, and how to die,
You taught me love, and self-denial.

You taught me many, many things on prayer.
You even coached me through my travails.

You planted seeds that helped me to grow.
Some you watered, as you would flow.

Sometimes I thought you did not care,
But now I know my life you bared.

While in your womb you one time said,
"You are my baby, God put you there."

I remember that day it was so hard.
I wanted to leave, and cut the cord.

But you cried out, with big bold tears
And told me "God sent you here."

Not all the time, did I understand,
The womb that God held in His hands.

That womb of yours has carried much weight,
From mighty women that you have birthed.

I give you honor, because it is due.
With lots of love, my heart says, "Thank you!

Daughter

9

From The Author's Heart

The pages ahead were written with tears from a heart of intercession that took every ounce of my being to bring forth. Every fiber of this book was birth from a vision within my spirit that was long placed there before I ever viewed the place called "*the nest*". Ironically, I was in the "*show me state*" called Missouri when I heard God speak to me concerning this vision. As the road of hard trials and struggle came my way, they forced me into the face of God, and caused me to seek Him with all of my spirit, body, and soul. This is where the pieces of the puzzle for the will of God began to truly unfold for me. It was impossible for me to think this up with my natural mind and have it work together. However, it was with the eyes of my spirit that God caused me to discern the seasons of my life. He gave meaning to them by using various analogies, as I experienced the power of true worship. *He that has an ear let him hear.*

Since I can remember myself, I have always experienced the presence of God around me. As a very young child, I was unable to express what I was experiencing due to my immaturity and the lack of knowledge of God and His ways. Although, these situations are true in their entirety, I must say that it was not until after I left "*the nest*," that God allowed this anointing for writing to come forth in my life. As I wrote each letter, word and chapter, I experienced powerful deliverance, and healing. My prayer is that the *overflow* will bless you, as well.

The meat of these chapters were written in a total of three, anointed days while sitting in the presence of the Lord. However, the finishing touches and rearranging was done over a period of three to four years. (Not only was this season finished on these pages, it was *"Finished"* in my life.) I wrote it in three days and *"Became"* it in four years.

I am not attempting to present this book the way that secular writers would present theirs. This book was written with the ink, and fire of God's love, the power of His Mercy, and the Strength of His Grace. I purposefully, prayerfully, and intentionally give Him all the glory for what He has done. With the strength of God in me, I pray that you will read it prayerfully, and with an open heart for change. Learn to "rest in the nest". Don't break the cord to your divine connection. Let God cut the cord. Breaking leaves everyone involved in pain. Cutting leaves peace. *Live out of the mouth of God!*

Key-Be

Contents

CHAPTER 1 ♦ I Will Provide For You A Nest

CHAPTER 2 ♦ The Eagle Called, "MOM"

CHAPTER 3 ♦ Under The Shadow Of His Wings

CHAPTER 4 ♦ Obstacles Are Your Stepping Stones

CHAPTER 5 ♦ When Judas Kissed Me

CHAPTER 6 ♦ Three Days In Hell

CHAPTER 7 ♦ The Fall Of Man Called, "ME"

CHAPTER 8 ♦ Don't Kill The Baby

CHAPTER 9 ♦ Do You Have Good Credit With God

CHAPTER 10 ♦ Piercing The Darkness

CHAPTER 11 ♦ God's About To Induce Your Labor

CHAPTER 12 ♦ Reservation In the "INN"

CHAPTER 13 ♦ Let The Waters Run

CHAPTER 14 ♦ The Recovery Room

CHAPTER 15 ♦ Freedom Under Fire

Thorns In My Nest

1

I WILL PROVIDE FOR YOU A NEST

"...And when they had platted a crown of thorns, they put it upon His head, and a reed in His right hand: and they bowed the knee before Him, and mocked Him saying, Hail, King of The Jews!   And they spit upon Him, and took the reed, and smote Him on the head.   And after that they had mocked Him, they took the robe off from Him, and put His own raiment on Him, and led Him away to crucify Him."

Matthew 27:29-31

CHAPTER ONE

I Will Provide For You a Nest

My child, step back and hear the Word of the Lord. Just as the father bird protects his young from all danger, I shall do for you. I will never leave you nor forsake you. Just as the mother bird feeds her young by gathering the worms and dropping them into her young's mouth one by one, I shall also do for you. I am your Provider. I will take care of you. Even as I have prepared *the nest* for your comfort, shelter and rest, I shall cause you to go from *the nest* to the branch. I shall see to it that you leave your nest, the place of comfort. You shall thrust out to the branch as if one in desperate desire to try his new wings. I shall move you from one end of the branch to the other. And suddenly your faith shall soar to another level and you shall take off from the branch.

Though some shall see you as one powerful in flight, it shall only be your beginning as I strengthen the wind beneath your wings.

I shall be your Wind. I shall be your Strength. When you run into obstacle after obstacle, I will suddenly throw you up higher and higher. I shall throw you up three times representing the Father, the Son, and the Holy Ghost. On your last thrust, I shall throw you up so high that it will cause you to soar up with wings as an eagle. You shall run and not be weary, walk, and not faint.

The Word of the Lord in your mouth will break the chains of darkness off of My people. They shall learn to trust and believe by your example. Demons of Poverty and Destruction shall be broken off of My people. Women and men will began to raise their standards. They will answer the call and seek after the will of God Almighty! I shall reward you with My goodness. I shall reward you with My rewards. For your life is My life, and My life yours. I give you all that you need to run the race. I say to you, trust in Me. I am your God. Seek after Me. You shall find Me. I shall give you secrets in My kingdom. You shall know things that others long to know of Me. Stay close.

"And I will give thee the treasures of darkness, hidden riches of secret places, that thou mayest know that I, the Lord, which call thee by thy name, am the God of Israel." (Isaiah 45:3)

I desire you as an offering for Myself. I love you! You are the end result of My work. I have the blueprint to what I have made and what I am making of you. I designed you to My taste. I made you for My enjoyment. I want you for Myself. I am a jealous God. Know that I love My time with you. Put or place no god before Me "I AM" the Lord your God. You will only find peace when I am your covering. Give no place to the devil.

Love *unconditionally!* Show mercy when it is time. Speak only My Word. Let your mouth be transformed for My mouth. Eat My Word for your health. Be careful to handle all that I give to you with care. Keep your focus on Me and Me alone. Revelations will be many. Stay humbly in My Presence. Always know that it is I working in and *through* you and not you yourself. Give or receive no glory for My work. I will share My glory with no one. Glorify Me! *I AM THE LORD YOUR GOD.*

Lonely, hurt, and rejected, I stood at the kitchen window struggling to clean every spot and speck as I prepared to move out of my military quarters. As I cleaned the window, I noticed a bird was pecking at the window each time that he saw me in view. He pecked as if he was attempting to attack me for some odd reason. It bothered me a great deal because each peck left a smear. The pecking went on so long that I stopped and it drew my attention to study the attitude and bold tenacity of this bird. He was audacious and fearless to the point of attempting to destroy me, as though I were a threat.

I watched his actions and admired his stance as he positioned himself with a very courageous stand. He presented a stamina that let me know that he would attack with great and deadly force if I got any closer. He showed a degree of potency and power as he struck the window, producing a quality of strength that left me stunned. He was so focused on me as being his enemy that his very eyes were like a sniper-scope. He was seeking me out. He was on the lookout.

I was quite perplexed and filled with amazement as my spirit began to soar and burn with fire as the Lord began to speak to me in a still, small voice. I gazed to and fro, up and down, when suddenly I noticed that there were two fragile birds in a nest located in a tree nearby. There also stood an adult bird on the branch dropping worms into the mouth of the two birds. As she dropped food into their mouths, they held their heads back and stretched their beaks wide open to receive their meals. Finally, it dawned on me that the bird on the lookout was protecting these young birds because he viewed me as a potential enemy.

Now that I understood what was happening, the Lord spoke to me and said, " *This is how I am going to protect you and this is how I am going to provide for you. Open up your spirit and receive My Word. I am going to place you in a nest, and I shall choose for you your food and cause you to grow. Trust me I am your Provider."* I immediately fell to the floor and began to cry out to God. I was overcome by an intense assurance of purpose and destiny for my life. I felt as though my every struggle had paid off. Not knowing then that someday I would be a living example placed on display for others to draw a sense of encouragement.

My life was tied to every thing that I viewed in the life of those wonderful God made creatures. In those birds I saw family, something that I longed for. I saw unity and love along with oneness of heart among them. I watched those birds daily until the day I left those quarters. Fortunately, I was there long enough to see them take off in flight. Each day, as they gained more and more strength, they slowly moved from within the boundaries and limitations of the nest and onto the branch. As the mother bird fed them, they continued to get more strengthened and even chirped a little louder. Eventually, one after the other, they made their way to the edge of the branch and then off they went into the air, flapping low to the ground. It seemed as if their wings were not strong enough to take them high.

On the last day that I was there, I stepped out of my car with my mind focused on the task that I was working on, as I noticed a bird flying towards me. I was overcome with fear because my human nature does not particularly desire to be close to any God created animals. Therefore, I screamed with a very loud voice, "A bird!" Just as I said that, the very young bird flew right into my stomach. When he landed, he was sitting right next to me looking all around.

Out of nowhere, a little boy, (whom I was not familiar with) came up to me and said, "It's just a bird, he only wants to fly." He then picked up the cute little critter and threw him up for flight. The tiny bird, struggling, after hitting a building, fell to the ground. The boy picked him up again and threw him up a little higher. Again he flew into the building landing on the ground in much fear. On the last throw, the little boy said, "*You have to throw him up with much might and then he'll fly.*" Finally, the bird took off in flight and left me standing there in tears.

When I turned around the little boy who was a stranger to my eyes, was gone. I knew that He was not from my neighborhood. He was certainly an Angel of the Lord. God said to me, "*That bird was you, and I am going to throw you up. Only I have the power to exalt you and display the character that I am about to develop within you. You may run into some obstacles (people), but you shall soar.*"

As we left that military base, disappointedly, I looked out of the window of the car as I traveled with my former husband and kids to Chicago. He had informed me that he wanted a divorce. With assurance I went, knowing that my destiny was in God's Hands.

2

THE EAGLE KNOWN AS "MOM"

> "So he departed thence, and found Elisha the son of Shaphat, who was plowing with twelve yoke of oxen before him, and he with the twelfth: and Elijah passed by him, and cast his mantle upon him."
>
> 1King 19:19

CHAPTER TWO

The Eagle Known As, "Mom"

As I began to drive down Lake Shore Drive in Chicago, I was overtaken by what I call a spirit of urgency to get God's attention. As the tears began to flow down my face, I spoke very softly and deeply to the Lord. I prayed! I told Him, "I will not stop driving this car until I hear Your voice. I have to hear You today, God. I feel like I can kill myself or just run this car into something." I wanted to die. The only thing I wanted over death was a voice coming from the Lord. It did not matter to me what He chose to say, just speak Lord. That was my heart. If His choice of words were "Boo", that would have been okay with me. I just wanted to know that God was with me. I was at the end of my road and had already let the knot of the rope slip through my hands.

God had promised me that I would someday soar, but I felt more like a chicken flapping than I did an eagle soaring. Suddenly, to my amazement, there came a sound in my spirit. I heard the Lord say, "The woman that you heard on the radio, go and see her, I have a Word for you." I remembered the voice of the woman, but I had no idea who she was or from where she had come. All that I could remember was I felt something go through me the first time that I heard the advertisement that she was coming to town.

While crying I asked God, "Lord who was she and what station did I hear the announcement?" The Lord spoke to me and said, "Turn on your radio." At the moment that I turned on the radio, there she was shouting under a very powerful anointing, **"God's going to move in this place tonight, I said God's going to move in this place tonight!!!"** Immediately, in my mind I began to sense hope. It was a hope that stimulated my hunger to have more of God. I was experiencing a "spiritual breakthrough" hope.

My perception changed. "This was the turning point." I was no longer breached, but was in a place to come forth as God planned. Just this little hope had caused my shell to crack and my desire for God's will to awaken.

Proverbs 13:12 says, Hope deferred maketh the heart sick: but when the desire cometh, it is a tree of life.

Hope is cherishing the desire, but it is not desire. Desire was coming for me. When my hope was restored, it produced within me the hunger and desire that's needed to be filled.

"Blessed are they which do hunger and thirst after righteousness: For they shall be filled. (Matthew 5:6)

First of all, the bible says blessed are they, "Not cursed." Hunger for God is a part of the process of breaking the curse of an impoverished spirit. (Spirit of poverty within your spirit, soul or body.) When the filling comes, the curse is broken. Even sinners must sense a void before they can get a fill. They must hunger. Then God will come in when they confess and believe in their hearts that Jesus is Lord. If you don't have God in you, then you are spiritually impoverished.

When I saw the word "Be", I knew by divine revelation that they, which do hunger and thirst...shall "Be" or "Exist" in the perfect will of God, with the filling of being satisfied and full of His power, holiness, and righteousness. In other words they shall be filled with "The Spirit of the Living God." To be filled with God is to be blessed. Filled means...

1. The overflowing of your spirit that's filled with God.

2. The Spirit of God in you flows over into the soul of you. (Your mind, reasoning, thinking and will.)

3. The Spirit of God that has totally changed your mind flows over into the body of you-your flesh. At this point, you don't do what you used to do, and you don't say what you used to say. You are "Sold Out!"

This equals filled when the spirit, soul and body of man is prospering. When you are filled, then you can flow over into the lives of others. You can "Be" filled. You can "Be."

"Be a key" and set the captives free.

To have a salvation and outer court experience is only 1/3 of the plan. To move on to the works stage in the holy place, and be totally committed to your local church is 2/3 of the plan. But to be holy in the "death to self" stage is 3/3 of the plan. This is the "God Only Dimension". This is the realm of being made whole. You become a single, whole individual. This is where holiness is a way of life and prosperity is inevitable. The "God Only Dimension" is where ministry is effective, witnessing is effective and anything that you put your hands to prospers. This is covenant promise for those that walk upright before the Lord – They shall eat the good of the land.

Hunger comes by hope, but the filling comes by faith. Hope deferred is equivalent to faith denied. Without hope I would not have moved on to faith. Without faith it was impossible for me to please my God.

Hope can be delayed by depression. Hope can be held up by past generational curses. Hope can be postponed. (By the people that you strive to please – called people pleasers). Hope can be rejected by rejection's spirit. Hope can be put off by a sluggard's spirit. Hope can be detained by discouragement. Finally, Hope can be stopped by stubbornness.

"But sanctify the Lord God in your hearts: and be ready always to give an answer to every man that asketh you a reason of the hope that is in you, with meekness and fear." (1Peter 3:15)

When I tapped into the gift of hope, I was able to say..."Now Faith!" Hope is cherishing the desire, but faith is the substance of things hoped for. Hope is cherishing the desire, but faith is the "evidence" of the things I could not see (Hebrews 11:1). As hope gushed from my sick heart, the fluids that surrounded me from within that shell were leaking as the waters broke forth from within my spirit and surpassed my flesh. As the radio announcer shouted, "Vedar Nichols from Port Huron, Michigan, tonight at 7:30", my hope came alive. I drove the rest of the way with hope.

As I drove home, I went as fast as the moving traffic would allow me. It was about 2:30 in the afternoon. I called on my mother to baby-sit my two children. I was dressed by 3:30pm. I walked the floor of my mouse and roach infested apartment for about two and a half hours praying and calling out to Almighty God. I heard the voice of the Lord say, " *Today is your day. You will never be the same again.*"

When I finally found the church that I was looking for, I noticed it was in a very large warehouse. It did not matter to me. I was ready to go to hell and back to receive the Word that God was to speak through the Woman of God. I knew that this meant my deliverance. I arrived around 6:30pm. I was the first to show up along with the people that were there to set up. I sat in my seat with a fire in my gut, hope in my heart, and a mission on my mind. This was my day. This was the day that I was to breakthrough, as if I was coming forth through a spiritual birth canal. Personally, I felt like telling everyone that showed up to go home because, this Word was for me. I knew that God was giving me His personal attention. The doctor was in the room to deliver my soul.

When the Woman of God finally got up to speak, she worshipped the Lord for some time and called me out. She said these words to me, "*God sent me here for you. You are a winner.*" She ministered some very precise things to me in which I will not mention. I was so overtaken by this divine intervention that I was launched into another realm immediately. She was one of the most powerful divine connections in my natural life.

God uses people to bring forth His will. Every person that you need to connect with will be set in place. God will use relationships that He has ordained to impart different anointings into you. When I met my mentor, I was locked inside of a *cracked shell* that was ready to be broken apart. All I needed was the right "environment of struggle" to allow me to break out.

The struggle is necessary to teach you how to "rest in mess" and depend on a friend-*Jesus.* I filled that shell to the fullest capacity. It was when my mentor and I connected and she spoke a powerful Word into my spirit that caused me to grow within a moment and the twinkling of an eye. It was enough to break my shell open. *For me it was a miracle breakthrough.* This is the power of the prophetic ministry.

Although I did not know her in the natural realm, I know that she was pregnant with me in the spirit. God had used her to birthed forth many women. There were many that she carried, yet she had not met. She simply had a burden for women like myself. My destiny was somehow locked to her.

God has your umbilical cord "connected" or "locked into" somebody, somewhere. The cord stays connected until it is time for you to come forth. When that time comes, God will **"Cut the cord, but He won't break the blood."** Never forget who your spiritual and apostolic parents are. Bastard children are fatherless. God is raising apostolic sons and daughters that will carry on the name in the family, the name, and message of Christ.

When you find your divine connection, stay in place. There will always be an Elijah waiting to drop a mantle on an Elisha. (As pastors and leaders you need to be careful, not everyone belongs in your church. You may not have what that individual needs to nurture what's in them. They may not have your DNA or spiritual genetic coding. I beg you to know the difference. Furthermore, God does not clone us, He sends people to nurture us. (Spiritually, your children should look something like you.)

My mission is to push people where they belong. If you do not belong with me, *"Get where you belong."* I must maintain a selfless attitude in mentoring individuals. It is not about personal gain and being seen. You must have a real heart to see people transformed in the renewing of their minds and changed in the depth of their hearts. Not everyone can mentor you. There is a great need for men and women to give their lives to mentoring within the Body of Christ. Mentoring is nothing more than personal discipleship. Go and make disciples of men!

Your God Shall Be My God

One of the nights during that meeting, Prophetess Nichols was leaving. The Holy Spirit said to me, "Go after her." By nature, I do not usually chase anyone. This was certainly out of my character. I have never felt so drawn to anyone in that manner. We were drawn to each other. It was not her that I was after, but it was what and who was in her. As I began to move quickly towards her, she turned suddenly as if she knew that I was coming. Suddenly she laid her hands upon me and began to prophesy. She looked me straight in the eye and said, "*It's going to cost you something.*"

On that night, she gave me the suit that she had preached in. God told her to tell me that the anointing on her life would be transferred to mine. He said, "*You shall receive a Double.*" As the anointing engulfed my being, it left me so drunk that I was unable to drive home.

The next morning, I found myself there in the hotel room with this prophetess that I had never seen before. I burned within my spirit as a tangible anointing shot through my body all night long. It felt as if jolts of lightning were surging through me. I did not sleep all night. But I was rested.

The next day I decided to wear the suit that she had given me. When I put the suit on, I began to experience a burning fire from my head to my toes. I could not speak. My spirit was so enlightened to deeper things in the realm of the spirit. My five senses seemed obsolete while my spiritual senses took total control. I was caught up. The fire of God burned within me with a mighty blaze. I knew that I was healed from any disease that thought it wanted to come near me on that day. There was a cleansing and purification that I experienced that blew my mind - it blew my old way of thinking. I was beginning to change for the purpose of the call of God on my life. I was anointed to serve. For approximately thirty days, I burned uncontrollably.

God had spoken to Prophetess Nichols and myself that she was to mentor me. From that time on, she became "Mom". Just as Ruth followed Naomi, I followed her. Her God truly became my God. Although I am from Chicago, my home became Port Huron, Michigan, "*The Nest*." Home is truly where the heart is, as well as the heat. That is the heat of His fire and the cloud of His presence. Stick with the glory cloud. Follow the flame and not the fame.

As I would travel with her from time to time, I was amazed at the example of Christ that God had placed in this earth, and most of all, in my life. She is a woman sold out to God, at all cost. She has suffered many things, including cancer of the lung, only to be healed miraculously by the Word of God. She is a woman of great character and integrity, which exemplifies the life of Christ. She will give you the clothes off of her back.

With all of these things that beautifies her wings in flight, she takes no junk off of her enemy, Satan. With the Word of God, she will rip through the enemy's camp, and will take her "beak" and rip it apart. When she goes go up in flight, you can see and feel the wind of the Spirit as it causes her to soar. This is the eagle that is known as "*Mom*."

The Nest

Just as a bird gathers dirt, mud, hair, trash and thorns to build a nest, it seems that God decided to create the same type of nesting environment for me. He placed me in the midst of gossip, clicks, and backbiting spirits. When I arrived, I did not view it as God's plan. I viewed it as a set up by the devil. However, God knew that it would provide a place for me to break forth out of the shells of my past. He knew that it would cause me to grow up and leave behind the broken pieces of rejection and hurt, that once held me captive. The thorns stuck me every once in a while, and helped break open my shell. When I got too close to the edge and wanted to leave *the nest* before I was able to fly, those thorns (the pain of the struggle) kept me balanced in the center of *the nest* as I rested in the palm of my Gods Hands. When the pain arrived, that's when I cried-*out to God*. When you learn not to struggle and kick against His will, divine rest is inevitable. The struggle is good for the breaking of the shell. However, at some point you must learn to rest in the nest.

You can be a nestling (a young bird that has not abandoned the nest). This is the Will of God concerning your life. Don't leave *the nest* before God's appointed time. There is an appointed time. Don't get off the Potter's wheel. He is the Potter and you are the clay. Whenever the Potter touches the clay, he creatively uses a finger or two to change the form of the clay. With every touch the Potter dips his fingers in the living waters (your own tears of intercession as you cry out to God) to give you moisture and make the process smoother. Although there may be pain involved in the touch, it is only to make you better. The touch is only given when there are changes to be made. *It's time for you to change.*

Change can be a painful process especially when you are faced with what's really going on in "You". *Changes are made to bring beauty to the vessel.* Humble yourself and lose the right to be right. You have to *DIE!*

"*And we know that all things work together for good to them that love God, to them who are "the" called according to HIS purpose.*" *(Romans 8:28)*

The thorns, the trash, the dirt and the mud will all work together for your good. The mess in *the nest* will cause you to be blessed. Let *the nest* house you until your time of maturity, until the whiteness of your head comes forth. When a bald eagle's head is white, he is mature. White also represents purity in the life of a Christian. God is purifying your temple. Let Him clean your house. He is Jehovah Kadesh-the God that sanctifies.

"Holy priest of God, you must stop at the brazen laver where the agent of use is water, and God reveals you to yourself as you look into the mirror of His Word. God wants to use the water of His Living Word to cleanse you. The contamination of your walk with God is not because of your personal sin, but because of what you picked up along the way as you were trying to please Him in your own strength. If you want to move on behind the veil of God, return to the brazen laver (the Word of God) and meditate on it day and night. You need God's Word to minister behind the veil."

WET WINGS CAN'T FLY HIGH

Obedient to the Lord, I took the few items that I owned, my two small children and moved to Port Huron, Michigan. When I arrived there, I did not realize it, but I had brought along all the baggage from my past. Within those bags were deep hurts, spiritual wounds, anger, abuse and massive rejections. Unlike an eagle, I had wet wings, and I was too heavy to soar. Eagles can only soar with lightweight feathers. Eagles use an oily substance to oil their feathers. This keeps the stormy wet rain from making them heavy in the air. (Like the eagle, the oil of God's anointing will cause the heaviness to roll off of your life. Weights and sins will be destroyed because of the anointing.)

One past situation that haunted me was an experience I had in the sixth grade, when my teacher beat me with a two by four and an extension cord. She did this continuously as the boys in the class held me down. I was very angry because my mother did not believe me when I told her. I felt extremely unprotected. I wanted my mother to help me. As a result, I went to live with my father temporarily. I ran away from home. It was when that teacher nearly broke my leg that I got my mother's attention. This left me bitter.

There were many other situations in my life such as, ungodly relationships (particularly from my high school days), abortions, divorce, etc., that left openings for demonic forces to hold me captive in my life. Wounded spirit, past hurts, and rejections were all generational curses in my biological bloodline. However, the manifestations of these spirits became obvious in my life when I arrived in *the nest.* It affected my relationships and my personality.

Not fully aware that I was entering *the nest* when I relocated, I had given my will over to the Lord. Therefore, it did not matter to me what was ahead, I wanted God's Will. God will use anything and any situation to make you, including your own selfish attitudes and weaknesses.

" Who hath directed the Spirit of the Lord, or being His counselor hath taught Him? With whom took He counsel, and who instructed Him, and taught Him in the path of judgment, and taught Him knowledge, and shewed to Him the way of understanding?"
(Isaiah 40:13-14)

While in *the nest*, the trash was the thing that housed me. The dirt was the thing that kept me on my face. The mud was nothing less than the dirt that God had mixed with His divine waters (tears of intercession) to give my nest substance. When you have substance, you have more stability and strength to stand in *the nest* or wherever He sends you. Substance is the weighty presence of God that comes to reveal and give you understanding.

This nest that God provided for me was not your normal church setting that was filled with mediocrity, complacency and tradition. It was filled with young soldiers and drill sergeants that made you quite mad when they tested your strength. It was a spiritual boot camp. Being a veteran of the United States Army, I understood with all of my being what that meant.

God was washing my brain with the blood of Jesus. He was brainwashing me. I needed a mindset and character adjustment. For what I had learned *"in the hood"* (past life before *the nest*), had a deep impact on my personality, thinking and daily choices. In laymen's terms, *"I was a mess, though not possessed, I was heavily oppressed"*.

"I beseech you therefore, brethren, by the mercies of God, that ye present your bodies a living sacrifice, holy, acceptable unto God, which is your reasonable service. And be not conformed to this world: but be ye transformed by the renewing of your mind, that ye may prove what is that good, and acceptable, and perfect, will of God." (Romans 12:1-2)

AN ORDER OF WINGS TO GO

The women that were around Mom at the time that we met were quite immature at times. I can remember times that they would gather themselves together in groups with much to talk about. Most of the time, I had no idea what the content of the conversations were. I was certain that it wasn't a good thing. Early on, I had overheard heated conversations that disturbed me. They affected me from the day that I moved to *the nest*.

I am sure these women wondered where did I come from. At times I would feel the rejection coming from them, but I pressed through in much deep, secret prayer. At times when I would leave their presence, I would go home and pray violently to keep from loosing my composure, as well as my mind. Mom always knew when I was being rejected. She also knew when it affected me the most. She'd comfort me in her own way, and encourage me in the Lord. Furthermore, she knew when all of her daughters were battling a demon. She was compassionate to us all.

Believe it or not, these "clicks" of division caused Mom to come under deep attack by the enemy when she was on the ministry field. Sometimes the hotel rooms were heated with demonically influenced attitudes in which we referred to at that time as "manifesting." I refer to them as "wings to go." There is nothing like a fresh set of cooked "hot wings."

The devil knew when her armor-bearers were not flowing in unity and therefore, it left her open for attack. When this would happen, she would rebuke, correct, lay hands on and dismiss the individual(s) for a season from traveling with her. Some were offended, but it was all about ministry. (The "hot wings" had to go)

Because this was not the time to be ministering to us, it hindered what God was seeking to do in those meetings. We got our personal ministry at home. We should have been prayed up, and ready to assist when she was on the field. Instead, some were competing for the position.

I did not know how to be an armor-bearer. I was watching and learning. Many times there were those who raced to carry the bible and the briefcase. All of this was new to me. I was in such need of healing that I could not find the time for a race. This is when I recognized the spirit of competitive jealousy. It was such an unattractive spirit. At one point, one of the armor-bearers made it her duty to let me know that she was called to be Prophetess Nichol's personal intercessor. The Prophetess never condoned these attitudes and she dealt with them as the Lord allowed her to see it.

The more I tried to draw into the women, the more I felt the blow of rejection. When I arrived in the nest, I felt like I had walked into the center of a war-zone. God was using it to shake me, to break me, and to make me. He used it to cause me to run to the face of God for acceptance. This was the purpose of the rejection. I learned this later as I went through deliverance from a root of rejection.

ELIJAH'S MANTLE

As I recall the last day of the meeting in Chicago, the message that Prophetess Nichols preached was, "Elijah's Mantle." It was a Word in season that God used to divinely connect us as mother and daughter. It was a Word that dealt with mentorship and being in the right place at the right time. At that time I did not realize it, but I was about to walk in an apostolic anointing. I was becoming an apostolic daughter of destiny. I was being delivered from the curse called "*The Bastard Child* (fatherless)." Because I was not raised in church, this was an intricate move in my life. I had finally connected with my godparents that were to pass on to me the heritage of the gospel. I was about to carry on the name of Christ.

I had learned quite a bit in the past few years from some powerful ministry gifts, but I needed that father's blessing and mother's nurturing touch. I needed some realignment, readjusting, and some corrections in my thinking, as well as some healing.

While in *the nest,* I wasn't always a difficult spiritual child. Once I knew the truth, I was ready to obey. (The truth can be a painful reality). One pastor in my past had told me that I had a deep unforgiving spirit. I disagreed, and I was a miserable sister. But, by the time I landed in *the nest,* I was tired of me.

Without mentoring I would have been a wild and loose bullet, shooting everybody in my path. I had no compassion and was an unmerciful servant. I could see myself blowing up everybody in the name of God, especially wicked pastors. I was waiting to eat them alive because I had been an abused sheep. Since the day that Mercy found me, He has taught me to hate sin, but to love the sinner. I can now show mercy, since it has been given to me. Compassion and Mercy is one of the most powerful gifts that my mentors flow in. It is in the mantle.

If you are going to get everything that God has for your life, "*You've got to be there when the mantles fall.*" You must be in the right place at the right time, "*submitted*" under the right covering. Too many of God's people are lone rangers and without proper covering, nurturing and accountability. You must be there in spirit, soul and body. You must be submitted to God and then to authority.

Mantles fall at appointed times ordained by God. You can never conjure up that moment again. It is only by the Divine Grace and Mercy of God. Elisha had to hang around Elijah to be there when he would go up. Elisha left everything to go and minister to Elijah. He left what he was doing for the will of God. (1 Kings 19:19-21)

The Bible says that Elisha ran after Elijah. Elijah had something that Elisha wanted. He had what he needed. When it came to the time that Elijah was to be taken up by a whirlwind, he told Elisha to, "wait right here." Elisha responded saying, "As the Lord liveth and as thy soul liveth, I will not leave thee," (2 Kings 2:2) then *they* went down to Bethel. Then he followed him to Jericho and Jordan. As they crossed over, Elijah asked Elisha, "What shall I do for thee, before I be taken away from thee." Elisha asked for a double portion of his spirit. Though Elijah knew this was a hard thing that his protégé had asked for, he let him know that "*If you see me when I am taken from thee, it shall be so unto thee; but if not, it shall not be so.*"

When the whirlwind appeared for Elijah, Elisha *saw it.* He was right there, in the right place at the right time. He caught the mantle *(2Kings 2:1-15).* Can you see? Do you have spiritual perception? The mantle falls when your mentor transitions to another level. When they go up, you get the mantle to move up to the next level, *if you can see.* The Key is to, "Get in your place and hook up with your divine connection."

God, I thank you for placing such a gift in my life. Though at times I was sick in the womb, Jesus kept me from aborting purpose and premature delivery. I thank you, Jesus, for using such ministering gifts such as Prophetess Vedar Nichols and Apostle William T. Nichols to assist in my birthing process. *I love you, Lord!*

Jesus, You are more than the world to me. You are my God! Your thoughts of me are so special. Your love for me is so great. Thank you for Divine Timing.

THIS IS YOUR NEST

This is your nest, the place where it's dark.
This is your nest, with the *"Family of God."*

This is your nest, the place where it's dark
This is your nest, to learn rest in *"MY"* arms.

This is your nest, where thorns find your heart.
This is your nest, where the struggle makes it hard.

This is your nest, where *"I* "told you to go.
This is your nest, to leave *I say, "NO".*

This is your nest, you must leave only by wings.
This is your nest, any other way is *"NOT ME".*

This is your nest, you can't leave in a shell.
This is your nest, the shells are holding you there.

This is your nest, you came here with your past.
This is your nest, you must shed it at last.

This is your nest, you came here with your hurt.
This is your nest, made of dirt, though it hurts, *"It Works!"*

Get free, be key and set the captives free!

Thorns In My Nest

3

UNDER THE SHADOW OF HIS WINGS

"He spread a cloud for a covering; and fire to give light in the night."

Psalms 105:39

Chapter Three

Under the Shadow of His Wings

can recall the days in the nest when darkness covered me. This darkness was so different from what I experienced when Judas kissed me (as you will see in the chapters ahead). This darkness had some sunny days. I was able to see, but it was limited to what was in and around *the nest.*

God covered me in my immaturity as He taught me to use my wings. He strengthened me with food that He so carefully and strategically selected for me. There were revelations that revealed only enough to keep me from choking. He knew my frail and weak body and understood just what a young eaglet like me could digest.

"He shall feed His flock like a shepherd: He shall gather the lambs with His arm, and carry them in His bosom, and shall gently lead those that are with young." (Isaiah 40:11)

I was forever feeling His fire, but randomly saw His light. Sometimes there was a flicker of light, but I thank God, it was *light*. My sight was not clear but my hearing was sharp. I was learning the art of listening. I use to pray and do all the talking, but now, I was learning to listen - *in quietness*. Understanding came as a result of what I heard. Clarity came as a result of what I understood. Clarity will always affect vision.

I could never understand why there was fire, but very little light. I mistakenly labeled this dark time of my life as, "of the devil." I thought all darkness was from the pit of hell and "not of God." It was after I left *the nest* that I began to understand that I was under the shadow of God's wings. Shadows are dark, even yours. Does that mean that your shadow is not of God? (Well, the dark side of God is found in His shadow, but He is Light and our sovereign King.)

His Word never failed to reveal to me the place that I was in. It was Jesus, my Great Eagle, whom I was looking up to as He covered me under the shadow of His Great Wing. Actually, there was Light everywhere, because He was there. However, my vision was not clear for my eyes were young. The Light was present and

He was that light. I was just on the side that His shadow was, being made in obscurity. *Know the difference between your dark times.*

> "Yea, though I walk through the valley of the shadow of death, I will fear no evil: for Thou art with me; Thy rod and Thy staff they comfort me." (Psalms 23:4)

In Psalms 23, the Bible calls it a shadow of death because it is *only a shadow.* There is the shadow of death, and there is death itself. There is also the Shadow of God, and then, there is God Himself, who is Light. In order to have a strong shadow, you must have strong light. I was in His shadow, what seemed dark was only my protection and covering. I was undercover! It did not look like I was going to be all that God said I would be, but I was being made on the dark side of the mountain.

Obscure in all things, darkness covered me. As a result, I was strongly misunderstood and ugly to be looked upon. I was hidden in Christ until I was to be revealed in the likeness of His dear son. The word of God says, that He will complete the work that He has begun in you until the day of Jesus Christ *(Philippians 1:6).* I knew that the Day or Light of Jesus Christ would come for my life.

I hear *you* asking, "God, where am I?" Well, child of God, it seems that in this night, this darkness, *this shadow,* all hell has broken loose. When you thought God should have shown up, seems to be the time He has decided to hide His face. His face is hidden because He wants you to seek Him while He may be found. *God* can be found, in the throne room (behind the veil). True worshippers Seek Him!

It is time to pray before you become prey. Relationships that you knew were divinely connected by God, seems to be disconnecting and utterly falling apart. (This is actually the process of God cutting the cord. Cords are needed when you are in the womb, temporarily.) All hope that you placed in people seems worthless.

God will separate you from every addictive relationship for the sake of turning your trust over to the Almighty God. Getting delivered from people is one of the most important and powerful deliverances that a man or woman of God can encounter.

To be used by God, you must be willing to put all of your trust in God, and God only. No matter how much you trust your mentors, God wants you to ultimately trust Him. No man shall get the glory that is due His name. While man will fail you, God will always be a Man of His Word. Since He called you, why not let Him be responsible for supplying the need? In the night, He desires to provide for you a Light-*Himself*.

I believe that God is so gracious that He covers us with darkness to deal with the very fibers of our character. This means allowing anything it takes to get you delivered from yourself, your *attitude,* and from people. *"Even after a fall (by God's Grace and Mercy) you can land in the Divine Will of the call."* God knew that you would choose to fall, so He had already planned for a set up.

Notice that when the cloud comes into your life, all issues of the past seem to surface. The cloud comes to bring a storm. The windy storm, have more than enough power to break open your outer shell. That outer shell can be your flesh or your past. A good storm will shake up everything. Everything seems to get on your last nerve. Though others may think you are strong, your strength is weakened. Your outer man may be dressed to kill, but spiritually you are torn, rejection posing as your best friend for the moment. No one seems to like your presence, just as no one seems to understand who you are.

Before the head of an eagle turns white, he is dark all over and ugly in all his ways. He does not yet know what to do with his wings. He is flapping like a chicken, hitting whatever and whoever else is in the nest. When you hear a person speaking out of turn and hitting others with words that lack wisdom, they are flapping. Their heart may be pure but they are destructive. Be patient with them, they are in training.

" Wisdom is the principal thing; therefore get wisdom: and with all thy getting get understanding. Exalt her, and she shall promote thee: she shall bring thee to honour, when thou dost embrace her. She shall give to thine head an ornament of grace: a crown of glory shall she deliver to thee." (Proverbs 4:7-9)

Could it be that the white head of an eagle is symbolical to the ornament of grace given to your head if you get wisdom and exalt her? Destiny awaits you. Your destiny is Wisdom. You shall be pure, holy and filled with the Wisdom of Almighty God.

Bursting forth in the seven Spirits of God, you are looking like the center shaft of the golden candlestick ~ *Jesus Christ*. The branches on the golden candlestick in the days of the tabernacle revealed God as Light. The six branches received oil (the oil of anointing) from the one taller shaft in the middle and were made to look just like the one in the middle. This is the church, and we should look like Jesus.

"And there shall come forth a rod out of the stem of Jesse, and a Branch shall grow out of its roots: And the Spirit of the Lord shall rest upon Him, the Spirit of Wisdom and Understanding, the Spirit of Counsel and Might, the Spirit of Knowledge and of the Fear of the Lord; And shall make Him of quick understanding in the Fear of the Lord; and He shall not judge after the sight of His eyes, neither reprove after the hearing of His ears: But with righteousness shall He judge the poor, and reprove with equity for the meek of the earth: and He shall smite the earth with the rod of His mouth, and with the breath of His lips shall He slay the wicked. And righteousness shall be the girdle of His loins and faithfulness the girdle of His reins." (Isaiah 11:1-5)

Bald eagles are not beautiful in the beginning. Their beauty comes in the end when they are matured. But remember, "your" end is not "the" end. *Your ending is God's beginning*. When you end (Die Out!), then God can begin (Live In You). It is the new place where the new you begin. In this stage you do things with good intention, but it always seemed to reap havoc all around you. It is only the Grace of God that will take you in the secret place and hide you under the shadow of His wings while He makes and breaks you.

God has a Divine Nightlight that will guide you in times of deep darkness. The darkest side of God (which is the side that His shadow is on) carries more Fire and Light than you may see. If there is a fire in the night hour, you will have no problem spotting the flame. Fire lights, because fire is light. Light causes eyes to see. When you can't see, *"just listen to His Voice". Be led by God's sound when your sight is bound. Experience the power of listening.*

Psalms 139

Thorns In My Nest

O Lord, Thou hast searched me, and known me.
Thou knowest my downsitting and mine uprising,
Thou understandest my
thoughts afar off. Thou compassest my path
and my lying down, and art acquainted with all my ways.
For there is not a word in my tongue, but,
lo, O Lord, Thou knowest it altogether.
Thou hast beset me behind and before,
and laid Thine hand upon me.
Such knowledge is too wonderful for me;
It is high, I cannot attain unto it.
Wither shall I go from Thy Spirit?
Or wither shall I flee from Thy Presence?
If I ascend up into heaven Thou art there:
If I make my bed in hell, behold, Thou art there.
If I take the wings of the morning,
and dwell in the uttermost parts of the sea;
even there shall Thy hand lead me,
and Thy right hand shall hold me.
If I say, surely the darkness shall cover me;
even the night shall be light about me.
Yea, the darkness hideth not from Thee;
but the night shineth as the day:
the darkness and the
light are both alike to Thee.
For Thou hast possessed my reins:
Thou hast covered me in my mother's womb.
I will praise Thee;
For I am fearfully and wonderfully made:
marvelous are Thy works:
and that my soul knoweth right well.
my substance was not hid from Thee,
when I was made in secret, and curiously wrought in the
lowest parts of the earth.
Thine eyes did see my substance, yet being unperfect;
and in Thy book all my members were
written, which in continuance were fashioned,
when as yet there was none of them.
How precious also are Thy thoughts unto me, O God!
How great is the sum of them!
If I should count them, they are more in number than the sand:
when I awake, I am still with Thee.
Surely Thou wilt slay the wicked, O God:
depart from me therefore, ye bloody men.
For they speak against Thee wickedly,
and Thine enemies take Thy name in vain.
Do not I hate them, O Lord, that hate Thee?
And am not I grieved with those that rise up against Thee?
I hate them with perfect hatred:
I count them mine enemies.
Search me, O God, and know my heart:
Try me, and know my thoughts:
and see if there be any wicked way in me, and lead me in the way everlasting.

The Lord would say to you this day, "My clouds are there to cover you. You are undercover. I have chosen to take you undercover to break you. I have chosen this way in order to prune you and reproduce in you My character and integrity. Though the cloud comes before the storm, I will cause the storm to carry you. Know that I am your God. I am the Fire in the cloud. I am your Light in the dark places. It is I that will burn through your character to purify and cleanse every evil desire and thought. Turn on the Nightlight, for I am your Night light.

Under the shadow of My wings shall I hide You. Your darkness will become as light to you. For, I will cause you to see into and out of the darkness.

"He that dwelleth in the secret place of the most High shall abide under the shadow of the Almighty."

(Psalms 91:1)

The very Fire of God will pierce the darkness that surrounds you to bring forth the breaking of day. Your darkened conscience will be cleared and the realm of your mind renewed and set free. I will not lift the cover until I burn through your will. In the midst of the cloud you will find My Fire. Let My Will be done in you as it is in heaven. Within your very being every valley shall be exalted, and every mountain and hill shall be made low: and the crooked shall be made straight and the rough places plain: And the Glory of the Lord shall be revealed, and all flesh shall see it together: for the Mouth of the Lord hath spoken it. (Isaiah 40:4-5).

Within your spirit is the Shekinah Glory of God. You are a carrier of the Ark of God. You are like walking mercy, walking fire, and an explosive, powerful force. You are "Armed and dangerous". You are a worshipper, one that worships in Spirit and in Truth. Undercovers carry very big secrets. You have the Divine Secrets of Divine Holy God within you. Under the cover, your Great Eagle "JESUS" will reveal to you secrets, in His kingdom. Let the darkness cover you.

MY SHELLS ARE IN THE NEST

(Leave the past behind)

My shells are in the nest.
Piece by piece they lay to rest.
Between the thorns that pierced my flesh,
My shells are there in the nest.
My shells are there, they are my past.
They lay inside the thorns at last.
They could never unite to become one again.
My shells are broken and at their end.

My shells they once held me tight.
They covered my eyes and blocked the Light.
They gave no space for me to grow.
They had to break to bring me forth.
My shells remind me of my pain.
They used to bind me as a chain.
But now they're gone and have no life.
They only live to *testify*.

Inside my shell there was a *Key*.
There was a *Key* to set me free.
The Key was *Jesus* who touched my mind.
He commanded me to
Leave it all behind!
Within a shell there is no light.
And it must break within your night.
You must not stay within your shell.
Within a shell there's always hell.
You shall break lose and try your wings.
God's Word commands that you will win!
In confidence and quietness strength shall come.
Do not be weary, don't faint, *"Just Run"*!

4

OBSTACLES ARE YOUR STEPPING STONES

"For verily I say unto you, that whosoever shall say unto this mountain, be thou removed, and be thou cast into the sea; and shall not doubt in his heart, but shall believe that those things which he saith shall come to pass; he shall have whatsoever he saith. therefore I say unto you, what things soever ye desire when ye pray, believe that ye receive them, and ye shall have them."

Mark 11:23-24

 61

CHAPTER FOUR

Obstacles Are Your Stepping Stones

I stood in the welfare line with tears in my eyes. I never wanted to go this way. I looked at my two small children as they continued to laugh and play. They had no idea that I was struggling when my former husband had taken us back to Chicago. His last words to me were, "Nobody wants you with two kids, all you are going to do is go to Chicago and live in the projects." I will never forget the day that he spoke those words. They pierced my being and began to operate with creative ability. I felt like prophecy was being fulfilled.

As I stood in that line I asked God, "Why didn't you make a way for me to escape this?" The Holy Spirit told me to stop and look behind me. When I turned around, there were drug addicts, alcoholics, hungry children, deceivers, whores, etc. You name it they were in that line on that day. They were of all nations. God said to me, "This is not only for you, this is also for them." I kept crying but the purpose of my tears changed.

"The voice of him that crieth in the wilderness, Prepare ye the way of the Lord, make straight in the desert a highway for our God." (Isaiah 40:3)

My deliverance simply meant someone else's freedom in the future. By the way, I was too proud for Uncle Sam's food stamp line. My pride had to go, because we needed to eat. A personal spirit of deliverance came over me. I had to feed my children. I can see why people in the bible got delivered after Jesus fed them. He got their attention. You can not give a hungry man God to eat! You must feed his belly.

When I arrived to the front of the food stamp line and my name was called, I asked the social worker, "Could you please tell me how to get off of this system, before I get on it?" I was determined that welfare was not going to be my personal address. I was not going to live there. It was only a transition. Immediately God told me to go back to school. I did just as he said.

When I arrived in *my nest* (Port Huron), I kept the same attitude. I received food stamps, moved into the projects on the worse corner in that city and I went back to school. While some were saying, "The Lord doesn't want me to work because I am called into the ministry." That never set right with my spirit. I eventually got a job. Working really taught me how to deal with people. God used my work environment to help develop godly character in me. I once read a sign that said, "Godly character is manifested in great moments, but it is developed in the small ones". Oh, how true.

I felt an urgency to do something for change. I ate very well with every food stamp that the State of Michigan supplied. I probably gained a few pounds, but I prepared myself to get a better job while being assisted. I spent them wisely as if I were spending millions in cash. Many times I shined my windows as if they were my own. I waxed my floors. I took the small thing that God had given me and treated it like it was big.

I tried to keep my housing project clean because, I had a vision of my own home. I scrubbed my floors, practicing to clean my own house that God was about to bless me with. I was able to get rid of the roaches in my apartment and the neighbor's too. The neighbor claimed that they had been there the entire five years that she lived there, and they were hard to get rid of. I wasn't planning on being there five years, and the roaches had to go. I had enough with roaches and mice in my past (with poverty comes a spirit of destruction and filth).

While others were moving from project to project, I was staying put until my change had come. Moving to another housing project was not my vision. Moving to another for me was not moving up, it was moving over and sometimes right out of the will of God. I was still blowing snot and crying, but I did it on my face before God. My communication with God was all that I truly had. My only comfort and hope was my relationship with Jesus.

At times *in the nest*, one of my covenant sisters and I would get out in the streets and minister to the drug dealers and the addicts. They would let us lay our hands on them for deliverance. Once, while we set in the Presence of the Lord, very quietly, a young drug addict knocked on the door. When I opened the door, the Presence of God was so strong that she fell on her face and began to go through deliverance. God told me to open all of the windows. When we finished ministering to her, drug dealers and addicts were standing in the windows and had been listening to the Word of the Lord that we were speaking to the young lady. God told me that we had planted a seed in every person that was listening. The young lady left that project with her hands in the air, crying out and praising the Lord. She walked down the street in that state.

As I gave myself in prayer and all that I had for the service of the Lord, the breaking in my life started in my mindset. This is where I had my greatest struggles. My old mindset is now a piece of the shell left in *my nest*. I had to change my mind by saying it. I began to speak what the Word of God said about my future. Your words are a powerful and creative force. I am not talking about positive speaking, but I am talking about speaking the Word of God to break generational curses. Even God, when he created the heavens and the earth, He spoke the Word.

The most important element in prospering is not material wealth, but spiritual and emotional wealth. Things will start to come as you first seek the face of God. His face is what you should want the most.

Within one year God had blessed me with a job. A journalist heard me talking with an optimistic point of view. She inquired of me for an interview. She came to my house and took my picture. When that article came out, it was on the front page of the Saturday paper. By Monday morning, a local bank executive called the newspaper after reading the article. They wanted to give me a job. A few days before I met this journalist, I told my pastor that God said that I was going to work at a bank. I saw it by the spirit. I started working that same week. Within thirty days, I was able to trade my beat up car for a new one. (My God is a Man of his Word!)

After working one year, I saved enough money to move out of the projects into a house (in which I rented) to have more room for a sister in the Lord that was living with me. God was progressively bringing me out, while at the same time developing my character.

I believe the day that I graduated from college something really broke off of my life. It was another piece of the shell that now lay in *my nest.* It was the shell of procrastination and failure. I had finished something. If you start something, you need to finish it. "A double minded man is unstable in all his ways." (James 1:8)

Many times, people blame others for their state of being. My favorite line was, "*the white man*". If the devil does not have power over you, what makes you think a white, black, yellow, or brown man does? God had to open my eyes of understanding.

"All nations before him are as nothing; and they are counted to him less than nothing, and vanity." (Isaiah 40:17)

Nobody can hold you down. I know that you can do all things through Christ Jesus, which strengthens you.

While I was trying to get off of the welfare system, I went back to school to prepare myself to do something. *Can you do anything?* You need something that you can do. While I was in school, I took advantage of many benefits made available to me such as babysitting funds, gas funds for my vehicle, etc. They even repaired my beat up car. I found out that asking questions can get things done.

The welfare system will help you if you want to be helped. It should be for transition not for habitation. You have to want to move up. A spirit of low self-esteem will keep you under. Fear is an enemy of faith. Fear is the enemy of creativity. Don't let your fears shell you in. You must believe God.

"He giveth power to the faint; and to them that have no might he increaseth strength." (Isaiah 40:29)

"Father God, in the name of my Lord and Savior Jesus Christ, I pray that Your people will get motivated by the right thing to bring change in their situations. I speak the Blood of Jesus against every sluggard and lazy spirit. I break the powers of darkness that would cause them to have major pity parties. Give them strength through the practical application of your Word. Balance them to do the complete will of God."

Many times our problems exist because we are not thankful. Be thankful. You cannot praise God and complain at the same time. And if you give, it shall be given unto you. You must learn to give out of your need. God has given us all something to give. Everybody has a *"Need Seed"*.

...AND FOR THAT SINGLE PARENT THAT FEELS, IT'S AN OBSTACLE IN YOUR WAY...

STAND...FOR YOU DON'T STAND ALONE

S...is for **"STAND"**, for you don't stand alone.
I ....is for **"I AM"**, who sits on the throne.
N...is for **"No Weapon"**, that is formed shall come in.
G...is for **"God"** in whom you shall trust in.
L...is for **"Long-Suffering"**, for the cross that you bear.
E...is for **"Endurance"**, because Jesus is there.

M...is for **"Much Prayer"**, to keep you sustained.
O...is for **"Opposition"**, yet strength for your pain.
M...is for **"Mother"**, you never gave up your role.
S...is for **"Stand, For You Don't Stand Alone!**

D...is for **"Dead beat"**, *No one can give you that name.*
A...is for **"Always Committed"**, and Jesus sees your pain.
D...is for **"Daddy"**, not many play this role.
S...is for **"Stand, For You Don't Stand Alone!**

5

WHEN JUDAS KISSED ME

"And while He yet spake, lo, Judas, one of the twelve, came, and with Him a great multitude with swords and staves, from the chief priests and elders of the people. Now he that betrayed him gave them a sign, saying, whomsoever I shall kiss, that same is He: hold Him fast. and forthwith he came to Jesus, and said, hail, Master; and kissed Him and Jesus said unto him Friend, wherefore art thou come? Then came they, and laid hands on Jesus, and took Him."

Matthew 26:47-50

CHAPTER FIVE

When Judas Kissed Me

Who knows the inner most secrets of your heart? Or who can encourage you in the deepest kind of ways? Who can lift you up when others tear you apart as if you were a lamb standing in wait to be slaughtered? Who can know you *almost* as well as you know yourself? Who can allow you to pour your very life into their very being as if you were they? Only one sent from God: *My Divine Friend.*

I laid on my face feeling as though the life had been sucked out of my bones during our Sunday service. Weakened from battle, I could not move. Without warning I was thrown into a desperate state of grief and mourning. Captured by my enemy, I was seized as a prisoner of war. Without a doubt, I was sure that death was knocking at my door. *It was my time.*

As I laid on the altar, church went on as usual while many tried the laying on of hands, encouragement of words, and hugs that normally were able to break the strongest yoke. I had never experienced such state of grief and separation.

I literally saw my body lying there as if one who had been wounded and shot down while fighting. Land mines of lies had been set up everywhere that I stepped. All around me there were explosions. Suddenly, *I was hit!*

My weapon was in my hand but I had no strength to pull the trigger. The trigger of my faith had been somehow disconnected from the firing pin that normally struck the Word forth within my spirit. My weapon was taken from my hand as I was accused of being the enemy.

The keys to my spiritual arms' room - *MY HEART* - had been confiscated. I had given them away in previous conversations with *"friends"* that I loved, as I would open myself up by sharing all that was within me. My life was wrapped up in those conversations filled with the revelations that the Holy Spirit had shared with me.

My future, my purpose, and my destiny were all under great fire, battle, and warfare. Spiritually, I had been suspended from life. I could not cry. I could not clap. Words were lost somewhere deep in the center of my gut. I had absolutely no one to call on, just an altar and not a single sacrifice to offer.

I knew that God was real, but for the first time in my saved life, I could not touch him. The captain of my soul, my Commander in Chief could not be seen. My spirit seemed to be separated from me. I had truly given up the ghost. All hell had come to chain me as I lay there dying a slow death...so slow, and my God, so long.

I saw highly ranked demons that gave orders to other demons to "Move Out!" They yelled at me while pain gripped my heart, while rejection wrapped itself around my neck. I was mocked and beaten with words of betrayal. Spit literally splattered in my face.

Slanderous lies were told on me. Lies that was so deep and entangled that it resembled that of a cobweb. A web so confusing that the slightest touch made it worse.

I was taken before the high priest of the house- *The Pastor and Eagle called, "Dad"*. The elders and all the council were assembled. Men sought witnesses against me, to put me to death. Though many were sought, no *true* witness was found. It was all a lie. But still, they continued to slash me. The wicked spirit of Jezebel had made her hit to take me out.

I had done no wrong. Along with lies, my inner most secrets had been uncovered and revealed. My deepest struggles walked upon me as I was accused of being a liar and a deceiver. I was made to look like the worst of enemies.

Out of the mouth of my friend came forth hatred and deep anger. "I hate you, I hate you," she screamed. *My God, What A Kiss?* I sank in my seat as I responded in question, *"why?"*

"A merry heart doeth good like a medicine: but a broken spirit drieth the bones." (Proverbs 17:22)

My friend was to me a special jewel, and a rare one. She, herself, had been formed through a process of irritating situations, as if she were a pearl in the making.

But, the fullness of time had come. It was time for the fulfillment of the Word of God in my life. It was time to cross over my Jordan. It was time to go through Calvary's way, "*the Cross*".

I felt many slashes and whips as the hooks of Jezebel entered my flesh. I had no cry that could be heard. It was a silent cry that made no noise. Deeply penetrated by every word spoken against me, I sank deeper and deeper into the grave. Dark it was, I mean very dark. Not one voice of the saints could be heard. No praise, no worship, just hell's yells! All forsook me and fled, even the ones that I knew loved me.

I forgot the "hallelujahs" of my past, and I had many. I forgot the battle march and how to march in time. The beats of the spirit were interrupted. I couldn't stand, I couldn't stomp, and certainly, I could not stay. For, it was time to go. *I decided to abandon my nest.*

I could not hear the former songs of the Lord's army, as we marched in time with steps ordered of the Lord, while singing his cadence. This militant worshipper was POW (Prisoner of War)!

The formation of my very being was shaken out of order. It was a true fall out. I could not answer to the call to, "fall-In." I could only fall out under intense pressure as the soldiers of Satan's army commanded me to stay down with their guns pointed at my heart and my head. They commanded my soul and I obeyed. They wanted to retrain me in their way and brainwash me for their kingdom. They wanted me to walk in cruel bitterness and unforgiveness against the saints of God.

There was only darkness, very cold darkness and this time with no light. This wasn't a shadow, this wasn't a wing, *"the lights were out."* I talked to no one because there was no one. I recognized other soldiers that had been captured, but I could not rescue them for I, myself, was held captive.

Above me were rounds of fire that appeared to be closer than they really were. It reminded me of boot camp, only this time it wasn't a silhouette, I was the target. Previously, I was the supply unit with many weapons for battle. I gave other godly soldiers guns to fight with, and I supplied them with rounds of revelations that would wipe the enemy out. (I was like an arms' room.) I had been trained to break a weapon down and put it back together within minutes. Spiritual M-16's, machine guns and hand grenades were my specialty. But, I was caught.

I remembered in basic training, I was taught to stay loyal to my country. I was trained to die for it. Well, here I was, I could not talk and I did not try. The enemy wanted me to curse my God and die. He wanted me to blaspheme His name and never speak it again. He wanted me to believe that God had set me up to die when He sent me a platoon sergeant-*My Mentor.* He wanted me to believe that my own fellow soldiers had made it their personal business to booby trap me. But, I made up my mind that I'd rather die than curse God or touch His anointed.

I can remember approaching one of God's highly anointed and well-recognized vessels, only to find myself rejected head on in the presence of many. All who were present knew and understood that I had just been rejected. There had been many other soldiers that had traveled through this particular war zone and was captured by the same demonic forces. It was as if demons had been lying in wait until the moment was just right. Though I wanted to talk, I could not say a word. *I had just received a divine kiss from a friend. It was a spirit called "Judas".*

PSALM 41:9-13

Yea, mine own familiar friend, in whom I trusted,
which did eat of my bread, hath lifted up his
heel against me.
But thou, O Lord, be merciful unto me, and raise me up,
that I may requite them.
By this I know that thou favourest me,
because mine enemy doth not triumph over me.
And as for me, thou upholdest me in mine integrity,
and settest me before thy face for ever.
blessed be the Lord God of Israel from everlasting,
and to everlasting. Amen, and Amen.

Alone and obscure I forgot what the anointing felt like. I couldn't see my Great Eagle, Jesus. Neither could I see The Eagle called, "Mom". In my throat, it felt like an obstacle was lodged there to keep me from screaming or breathing. In the darkness, I met my old buddies like fear, rejection, anger, hatred, bitterness, lust and failure. Failure had become a very big girl. She had grown to the point that she was like "a giant in the land." Very mature in form, she actually deepened my fear. Every part of her body was in form, as she seemed to lay her hands upon my head. It felt as if failure was imparting herself into me while raping me of my courage and faith in God. She impregnated me with great fear. I could not hear my God, for Satan screamed in my ear with laughter.

Darkness had a job. It worked to death. Darkness employed demons giving them positions to control my mind (witchcraft). They were paid big to capture me because I was worth something in God's kingdom, even though at the time I only handled small arms in the spirit. They knew that if I stayed alive, that I would someday be promoted in the high ranks, coming forth like a deadly atomic bomb shaking the foundation of territorial demonic forces. They also knew that I was destined to be "Armed and dangerous." They followed orders and were strategically set up with plans to manufacture my soul and reproduce for itself—my *death*.

The enemy told me that I would never be used of God. He told me that I had no purpose. He said, "*You are going to die.*" As I struggled in my body, the disease that had attached itself to me sent me off in deep pain as I eventually faced major emergency surgery. He knew that I feared death. I heard lie after lie as he prophesied to me in his own *black* tongue of death. Deep within me I held on to something that sounded like a small but extremely faint whisper, "*It ain't over until God says it's over.*"

> *"Behold, the Lord God will come with strong hand, and His arm shall rule for Him: behold, His reward is with Him, and His work before Him."* (Isaiah 40:10)

I believe that I was somehow holding on to my mantle. When I left *the nest*, I got rid of everything that reminded me of it, except a suit from The eagle Called, "Mom". She had given it to me in the hotel room. It was now symbolical of my *mantle*. She had given me many things, but this one thing was for me. I could not give up what it represented. To let go of this was to let go of my purpose, my anointing, and my destiny-*my life*.

Having been concealed, hidden, and tormented, for the next fifteen months of my life, I walked through this place called hell. It was the darkest time that I had ever experienced.

I recently heard one of my covenant sisters (Prophetess Juanita Bynum) speak at our spiritual parents church in Grand Rapids, Michigan. As the Lord used her to bring forth His word, it gave me understanding in an area that I had been struggling with. She spoke of the blackness that she stepped into as she left from under their covering. She explained how she came into great darkness and fell into sexual sin when she left Port Huron, Michigan (*the nest*) nine months too soon. I had never considered the fact that I had left *the nest* too soon. Ironically, I had just mention to Prophetess Bynum while in conversation with her at the airport, that

I knew it was time to go-when I left. I honestly thought that I'd left on time. I was deeply wounded from a betrayal. Furthermore, I did not know how to handle the impact of the rejection that I was experiencing. As a result, I made the grave mistake of abandoning *the nest.* This was my disobedience.

When I looked at the facts and allowed the Lord to use her to bring light, I came to the conclusion that I had made the same dangerous mistake. *I broke the cord, instead of letting God cut the cord.*

There was a particular covering that we both received while under their leadership. Certain things were not a struggle, as long as we were connected and covered. This was the covering of an apostolic father. When we broke from the cord too soon, this left us both open for demonic attack by the enemy. Although, this was at different times in both of our lives, we had the same result of falling into sexual sin.

As for myself, it was a strange experience for me to leave *the nest* and walk into darkness the way I did, because I was not struggling with sexual sin at that time. (The enemy is waiting in the dark to deceive you.) As a matter of fact, I was focused and had finally found that place of contentment. Now I realize that my apostolic covering was also a divine protection, when I was walking in submission and obedience. (Let me inject a very important statement at this point. My apostolic parents were not walking in deliberate wickedness. They were not in adulterous relations, nor were they deceiving their children through control and manipulation. They were "parents in the Lord" not of darkness.)

When I reconnected with my apostolic parents, the blessings from my father began to overtake me. I had to forgive and get back in place. You have to know who your father and mother are. You have to stay connected, until God cuts the cord. You can't survive as a lone ranger. The enemy is afraid of your spiritual lineage. Don't leave the nest before your God-appointed time. Stay connected! (If you've broken the cord, remember cords dry up and fall off anyway.) Go back home "Prodigal Son!"

Everybody needs a Judas. Everybody needs his divine kiss. It is the thing that pushes you off the branch and onto the cross. (I should have gone to the cross when I was kissed, not to the grave and certainly not the belly of a great fish, as Jonah did). The kiss was the indicator that it was time to be crucified.

Judas is not a person. It is a spirit that seeks the opportunity to betray a trust (opportunist have Judas spirits). Before it betrays, it makes deals with those who have power over you. It is related to a Jezebel spirit in the sense that it is covetous. Judas will trade you for whatever it is he's seeking to get. (*Some of you are seeking fame, be careful, the spirit of Judas is about to overtake you, Seek God's face, not only His hand*).

When that spirit shows up, it comes with a militant unit called "*the great multitude.*" They pack swords and staves for your death. It is a coward spirit that will not face you alone. However, you must remember, the spirit of Judas will *hang himself.* Don't fight the kiss.

Your Judas may be in the form of a divorce, in the betrayal of wedding vows or it may come through a broken promise. The kiss of Judas will only come through those closest to you and will use someone that you truly love and trust. Judas can be as close as the one that shares in your meal at the dinner table.

The devil needs a natural body to carry out his work. It is not the individual that he uses, that deserves a blow to the head. It is Satan and his imps.

Regardless of the vessels used to cause pain in my life, I still had a responsibility to forgive and love. Jesus said, "Forgive them Lord, for they know not what they do." He still loved and died for them. He even died for Judas. I did not feel like forgiving, but I made a conscious decision to do so. My forgiving others was my personal choice. God had invested too much in my life for me to go out because of a kiss. I cannot and will not be held captive by my past hurts. *My shells are broken and lay in the nest.*

Also, it does not always mean that the relationship will be the same, but you must reconcile yourself to your brother or sister, If possible. Love covers a multitude of sins. Even if they do not receive you, you must humble yourself. Humility means death to the flesh. I have new relationships that I have to encounter. I have more visions and dreams now, than I have ever had. I am dealing with purpose and destiny and nothing will stop that. Because of the blood of Jesus, I can trust again. God has given me more wisdom, so now I can certainly trust again. The Bible tells us...

"Moreover, my father, see, yea, see the skirt of thy robe in my hand: for in that I cut off the skirt of thy robe, and killed thee not, know thou and see that there is neither evil nor transgression in mine hand, and I have not sinned against thee; yet thou huntest my soul to take it. The Lord judge between me and thee, and the Lord avenge me of thee: but mine hand shall not be upon thee. As saith the proverb of the ancients, Wickedness proceedeth from the wicked: but mine hand shall not be upon thee."
(1Samuel 24:11-13)

When Saul was delivered into the hand of David after running from him, he had all the opportunity in the world to rip him apart. David, in this case, was not an opportunist. David arose and only cut off the skirt of Saul's robe. He was convicted in his heart for doing that. The Lord forbid that he should do such a thing to his master, the Lord's anointed. David would not touch Saul because he was anointed. God's anointed is God's anointed, even when they come with a flaw and even if they come like a Saul. I have had more than one Saul in my path, but I can't put my hand upon them. I've even had more than one kiss from Judas.

Forgiveness is needed greatly in the body of Christ. We are the Light of the World. The world is looking at us. Should we preach it and not live it? I have suffered much pain from my own family in God, but that does not mean that they are no longer a part of me. It is called sibling rivalry.

My natural sister and I fought like cats and dogs when we were growing up. We fought over anything and everything. I still love her to this day. We cut the cord and went our separate ways in life, but we did not break the blood. Blood is deep and blood is powerful. I will not cut my sister off because she has failed me. Let me repeat that, "*cut the cord, but don't break the blood.* You cannot change the fact that they are your sister or brother.

Have you ever wondered, how many friends did you kiss before you were smacked on the cheek? Whatsoever a man soweth, that shall he also reap (Galatians 6:7). Before I knew what I know now, I had kissed a few myself...and saints, we are in covenant. Covenant relationships cannot and should not be broken. Are we willing to die for one another? A covenant partner will die for you. A covenant is of blood. It was a great death that Christ died just to fulfill His commitment to us, so who are we? We must also die one for the other. I will not throw my trust around to just anybody, but neither am I afraid to trust again. I, first of all, trust God. Relationships are needed in order for us to relate one to another. I value covenant in a deep way. When I see covenant, I see the blood of Jesus. Covenant is the binding of two into one. We are one in Christ.

I count it a small thing to die compared to the Glory that shall be revealed for my suffering. I also count it a small thing compared to what I have gained from my covenant brothers and sisters in Christ, prior to a betrayal. It takes the power of the Holy Spirit to get you to focus on the good and do away with the bad.

This does not mean that we cannot confront issues and deal with problems. Just as Jonathan covered David and hid him, we must cover each other even to the point of hiding each other. Don't uncover your brother. That is God's job. Expose the devil, but cover your brother. Those that are spiritual should restore such a one.

Don't let the small things distract you from the big picture. God has a plan. You would be surprised at the innocence of many saints who did not realize that they were in betrayal of a trust. Certainly there are those who are very aware of their actions. I would say to you, *repent.* Satan has a way of manipulating the saints of God among each other. It's *Witchcraft wrapped up in a Jezebel spirit!!!*

Somewhere intertwined you will find that a root of bitterness or a seed of jealousy causes us to war one against another, especially with our tongues. The book of James is a good book to read if you have a problem with the tongue.

"If any man among you seem to be religious, and bridleth not his tongue, but deceiveth his own heart, this man's religion is vain." James 1:26

When the kiss of the spirit of Judas smacks your cheek with great betrayal, know that your time has truly come. Your Judas will always come before your cross. Your cross will always come before your grave, and your grave will precede your resurrection, "*A kiss, a cross, and a crown*".

Before power and life comes into your ministry, weakness and death are sure to reign. The only kiss in this life that will launch you into destiny is the divine kiss of Judas. Tell your Judas to bring it on. *The kiss is okay!*

LETTER TO MY FRIEND

Dear Friend,

I am pleased in my spirit to have found you. I love you as Jonathan did David. **1Samuel 18:1** *And it came to pass, when he had made an end of speaking unto Saul, that the soul of Jonathan was KNIT with the soul of David, and Jonathan Loved him as HIS OWN SOUL. Then Jonathan and David made a COVENANT, because he LOVED him as HIS OWN SOUL. And Jonathan STRIPPED himself of the ROBE that was on him, and gave it to David, and his GARMENTS, even to his SWORD, and to his BOW, and to his GIRDLE.*

In other words, whatever was Jonathan's, it was also David's, including his warfare. You have my robe, my garments, my sword, bow, and girdle. I'll fight for you, friend. You are a special jewel to me. I love you with the love of the Lord.

Our relationship will certainly be different because we are not who we used to be. Nevertheless, I will not remove any fault from the enemy and what he's done between us. I've had my Saul's chase me for the sake of murdering me, but my Saul's were all anointed of God. I can't put my hand on the Saul's of my past. I forgive all of God's anointed. Vengeance is the Lord's. I hope that the Lord will certainly not repay anyone except Satan himself. I hate him with a perfect hatred.

I want to see your face. Old things have passed away and behold all things have become new. If you need pieces to completely heal, I'll give you what I have for the sake of healing only. I could hear in your voice that there was still something that you needed. Forgive them all, my friend, for they know not what they do. I will not sit back and allow the enemy to torment you without the fight of my sword and bow on your behalf. What's mine is yours. Remember? I know that you suffered many disappointments and hurts. FORGIVE!

When I got the word that you were not in Port Huron anymore, I was concerned. I had a need to find you. I remember the day that I came to get you from Chicago. I will never forget that. I can't protect you from all that you have a need to go through, but I certainly have a spiritual responsibility to help you heal and move on. You have come a long way. With the help of the Holy Spirit, you shall come forth!!!

I can't put in words the pain that I suffered when I left Port Huron. My wedding, the birthing of my daughter, the witnessing of my wedding vows, it was all done in loneliness. My heart was broken. My husband was such a soft touch and comforter for me. But, I had no one other than Audrey. My mother had a stroke and was in the hospital. My family was tied up with that. My friends were no more. I was happy but, I was sorrowful and down. The blessings were all around me, but I could not enjoy them. Money was there, things were there, but my covenant friends were not. A complete emptiness filled me to the point of death. Death was tasty for me. I wanted it. I felt that there was nothing else to live for. I cried on my wedding night because this is not the way I planned it. My husband was the perfect mate, but I wanted to go out with a bang. I can't change the past. God has restored and given me great joy. I don't want to go back to "The Nest", but I miss the eaglets that shared it with me. I love you.

KEY-BE
APRIL 23, 1999

Thorns In My Nest

6

THREE DAYS IN HELL

"There is therefore now no condemnation to them which are in Christ Jesus, who walk not after the flesh, but after the Spirit."

Romans 8:1

CHAPTER SIX

Three Days In Hell

)stepped into the room. Sitting before me were the women that I had so truly learned to love through the death of my flesh. I moved forward almost as if I was walking in slow motion. The moments were long and bitter. Faces present seemed to be right upon me, as I lifted one foot after another. I could feel in my spirit something bad was about to happen, *still I proceeded-overriding the warning signs.*

The Eagle called, "Mom" had taken me to speak to my sister in the Lord-Prophetess Bynum. As Mom waited outside in the car, I went in with courage. This took guts for me to do. As I stepped before this tightly knit group of women, my throat was knotted with a blockage of words as I hesitated and struggled for something to say. I could feel the intense pressure of the battle, even before I walked into the house.

Never had I experienced such a fight. I was not expecting a large crowd to be present. It felt like the "great multitude." I felt double-teamed, even though I was not there to do battle. I'm not sure if that was understood, because there were many *opinions* of who I was. This I knew.

Not knowing exactly where to start, I began to speak reluctantly, with the request of speaking to the one in the middle-my *spiritual sister Juanita*. She had come home to visit.

It reminded me of the times when I was younger, and my older biological brother would come home to visit. He was a basketball star, and we would watch him play on television every year. He was always in the newspaper, and in the spotlight. His visits at home were special to the younger kids in the family, because he was our big brother. This was the same tone in Port Huron-*the nest*. Prophetess Bynum was the big sister that we had watched on TV.

I was not there during her nesting days (or shall I say-spiritually, I was not born yet), and several years had passed since she'd left *the nest*. When I came on the scene, she was not very popular in the Body of Christ, but she was on her way. Because I was the new kid on the block, I behaved accordingly – like any new kid trying to find her place.

The family was very excited to see her. She had not been home for a while. I could see the enthusiasm and excitement as they gathered with great joy. That whole weekend was totally different from what I was used to seeing in *the nest*. It was like a homecoming or family reunion. On that particular weekend, I had been in *the nest* for several years.

I had been told about numerous family events that had occurred in the past. Some of the memories included Prophetess

Bynum. Over a period of time, I was given the family history without limitation. Some of the memories were sad, some were exciting, and others were funny. Nonetheless, It was our own account of family historical events.

Everyone had a particular place in the family tree. I was still searching for myself and who I was. I was trying to understand how I miraculously landed in this nest. Was I adopted? Was I engrafted in? Was I a foster child? There were tons of questions going on in me, and I was waiting to understand. However, I know that it was God's arrangement.

I found a sense of contentment through prayer and communion with God. Mom helped me because of her compassion. Dad strengthened me because of his mercy. It was the right place to be in. It did not feel right to my flesh, but it kept me on my face before God.

This whole nest and family presented a challenge to me that I had never experienced. (If your present church doesn't present a challenge to your growth, you are in a comfort zone. You will never reach your full potential in ministry or in God.)

A Lesson In Sign Language

As I stood before these women, I requested to speak to Prophetess Bynum. Before I knew it, I was talking *"to the hand."* In other words, she put her hand up to let me know that she was not interested in conversing. Her hand spoke many words, as one using sign language. For the first time for sure, I understood *"hands that talk"*. Her heart was in her hands.

As her hand went up, she uttered out of her mouth, *"I am not there"*. Out of the abundance of her *heart*, her mouth spoke. Furthermore, out of the abundance of her heart her *hands* spoke.

She had no idea that the enemy had just used her mightily. I was like a crushed bird, floating in the midst of the broken shells that housed me. I certainly was not expecting her to do that. All attention and focus was geared in the direction of that encounter. Rejection!!!

In the past, I had actually had thoughts of seeing a moment like this, as if God had already shown me that it was sure to come. I hoped that what I had felt was wrong, but it was not. I saw this before it happened, but it had to happen. However, I refused to accept it as a moment, to be revealed in reality. I was totally shocked.

ALL FRUITS HAVE ROOTS

As I returned to the car of my mentor, she asked, "Did you speak with her?" I told her what happened, and even she was alarmed. I could not cry. I was too hurt. (I cried five years later in the arms of Mom, as I asked her, "What did I do to her?") Like any mother, she was always concerned about the divisions between her children. (Mama knows best!) When you have so many children, sibling rivalry is inevitable in the child developing stages. Especially, when they are all talented, gifted and strong willed.

I believe that we all complained about each other to Mom at some point or another. However, she always addressed the issues of rejection, competitive jealous, insecurity, and the idea of feeling threatened by each other. We were taught to recognize, and handle wars within ourselves through the death of our flesh, and through forgiveness. Sometimes I hated to hear this, but I strongly respected Mom's counsel.

After that encounter with Prophetess Bynum, and for the first time, I truly experienced an extremely strong sense of abandonment, in the Body of Christ. I read somewhere that abandonment is an intensified form of rejection. I was left *alone*. I did not spend the weekend with the family, when our big sister came home. Ironically, that was also the last day that I was with my mentor, after the kiss of Judas. (Several years later we were reunited in the City of Brotherly Love-*Philadelphia*).

Somehow within me I felt abandoned by Mom (Much of my anger was geared towards her), since "I felt" that she birthed me into this new family of mine. (Later God had to remind me that He ordered my steps, not man.) This was the fulfilled vision of the "family of birds" in *the nest*! She and dad were my divine connections. I wanted her to help me, but she did not, and now I understand that, she could not. I believe that I would have stayed in *the nest*, had she come after me. I respected her that much. I would have also responded to dad, because he was so merciful. Unfortunately, I suffered a terrible wound of abandonment, a sense of homelessness and rejection. I truly felt that this was my sign to leave. (Though I was wrong). I ran away from home.

For some reason in which I did not understand at the time, all forsook me and fled. However, God had a strategic plan. He wanted to deliver me Himself. He wanted to get to the root of my rejection, not the fruit. Fruit is what you see with an open eye. The root is always hidden in the darkness of your past.

Isn't it strange how the enemy will always let you see things that hurt you, but he covers things that heal you like-*your past*. He will only allow you to see your past, if it will hurt you more. It takes the power of the Holy Spirit to reveal, so that you can heal. *Focus on healing from the root, if you want to see good, fresh and healthy fruit.* (Certainly God will be glorified in this.)

Here I was, faced with this vicious cycle of running away. It felt like a cycle in my life. My childhood issues had resurfaced. I had seen this before. I was mad at Mom, because she did not protect me. It brought back painful memories of the beatings that Mrs. Wilson would give me, in the sixth grade. I hated her. I was indulged in that hatred, passionately. I had planned to go back and kill her daughter when I got in high school. However, I had found out that she was no longer there. These feelings came back to haunt my mind when I felt unprotected by my spiritual parents.

During the wilderness days, after I left the nest, I had the God appointed opportunity of talking to my biological mother. Without understanding why, I began to talk to her about Mrs. Wilson. The conversation bought tears to my eyes. I told her that,

"I have no reason to lie, now that I am a grown woman. The woman beat me and lied on me constantly. She would take my money and send me home to get food out of our cabinet, and bring it back to school. We never did work in her class. I learned nothing in sixth grade, but hatred and abuse."

I was grown and still trying to prove to my mother that this woman beat me. Every time I would feel rejection, I would regress back to this particular child abuse incident. The hurt had returned.

I even had thoughts of my mother saying that she never wanted thirteen children. I connected these thoughts. I came up with the conclusion that she never wanted kids, and that's why she did not care when that woman would beat me. That was mental torment. That was also rejection talk. Rejection has its own language. If you learn the language of the demon, you can catch him when he speaks. Don't let him talk too much, CAST HIM OUT!!! Tell him to "GO" in the name of JESUS!!!

As a result of these feelings and manifestations, I eventually found the entry point of the spirit of abandonment and rejection. It had nothing to do with the people in *the nest.* It was from this terrible childhood experience.

I was able to get to the root of the rejection with loving help from the Housekeeper-Jesus. I had not forgiven my mother, for not protecting me. I had not forgiven Mrs. Wilson, who was an authority figure in my life. My wet wings, were no longer heavy, wet feathers. Finally, the oil of the Lord had been rubbed on my feathers. I found the root and cut it out with forgiveness. It felt like I had plucked out loose feathers and was able to soar a little higher. The heaviness lifted, and the pain rolled away. My healing had finally come.

Had I known where Mrs. Wilson was, I would have confronted her personally and forgiven her. I was told that she recently died. *God bless her children and save their souls.*

My mother simply trusted my teacher, like any mother would do. By the way, Mrs. Wilson put on a good front in the presence of parents. She fooled my mother and many others.

My perception was formed from my painful experiences with this teacher. I did not know how to judge my mothers decision to believe an adult, over a child. I was a child, with a child's mind. I had formed a thought pattern about how mothers should protect their children, based upon my experience. This affected my perception, and it made me who I was–*hateful.* (This was perceived rejection) I was now transforming these feelings, perceptions, and thoughts to my spiritual parents.

"For as a man thinketh in his heart, so is he..." Proverbs 23:7

I had certain expectations from Mom (my mentor), based upon a bad childhood experience. This was not fair in our relationship. It came between us. It produced death.

It was important for me to find the entry point, where the enemy planted a seed. I had to not only forgive, but change my perception and thinking by renewing my mind with the Word of God.

I found the entry point at age thirty- eight. This happened at age eleven. This was a full-grown seed. It brought forth death. It was killing my relationships. It was killing my ministry. It was killing me. When sin is full-grown, it produces death (James 1:15). Before God resurrected Mom and my relationship, it was murdered by the spirit of rejection-The Purpose Killer."

I can spot rejection in children. I am so sensitive to it. I see kids all the time that I want to hug and love. Most of the time, they don't know how to receive this love. That makes my heart hurt.

I try to pay close attention to my own children when they are hurting, as well. I can see the effects of the divorce in the life of my two oldest children. It has had a ripple effect. Although I was healed, they are now facing issues and asking painful questions. I see the entry point of their rejection and I am dealing with it in prayer, the Word of God, and the Blood of Jesus. I never want to see anyone carry a wounded spirit, rejection and hurt for 27 years, the way I did. I am being healed, as I write.

MY WORST ENCOUNTER

As we venture back to the encounter with the women, understand that one sister did try to correct me when I ran away from *the nest*. She was very harsh in her dealing with me. She was an individual who had no good track record in love. Her *lack of love* pushed me farther away. Rejection is cast out by receiving love- "The Love Of God." I was suffering from a deep wound of rejection that could only be broken with true love, in which I have found to be in Jesus alone.

Before this time, I was not rebellious towards my leaders. I was submitted to them. This left the whole situation a mass of confusion. God is not the author of confusion.

As time went on, it was revealed to me by God, that the spirit of Jezebel had invaded our spiritual family-we were warring within. That spirit came through and used all of us against each other. Because this was, and still is a deliverance ministry, I am not surprised. I have a deep hatred for this spirit, as well. A Jezebel spirit loves to destroy divine relationships and kill prophets. It always seems to have a lot of confusion and deception in the midst. It keeps stuff going on.

When I walked in the room where the women were sitting, only to be rejected, there was a total and complete unholy silence. The voices of demons raced in the atmosphere creating laughter and mockery of me with great joy, as if they had waited for this moment. The spirits gathered themselves together in deep unity as they spoke saying, *"We hate you! We hate you"*. It was one voice, one sound and one spirit. I knew that what I was feeling was real, because it manifested itself in the open two days later.

When Prophetess Bynum returned to *the nest*, it happened to be the same weekend that I experienced the betrayal by a close friend, as I mentioned in chapter five. (I was shipwrecked on that weekend) I know this was a strategic move well planned, and thought out by the enemy. Warfare is strategic. Satan's strategies are well planned out and ordered through his own chain of command of demonic forces.

Just as Judas had the bag in his hand when he approached Jesus, he had the bag in his hand when he approached me. What Judas had in his bag was cursed blood money. He had already assembled himself in the palace of the high priest. The plot was to arrest me in some sly way, and kill me off, with the idea of me never returning. These demons that were speaking wanted to stop my destiny. Physically, the women in the room never spoke a word. I only heard the voices of demons, as they tormented my mind.

As I was rejected in *coldness of heart,* my heart sunk! I had done nothing to my sister, at least not to my knowledge. She is my sister that, I truly love. Coming forth *before* me in the same nest, I looked up to her with great respect. Her courage to soar at that time was awesome to me. Her flight reminded me of the two birds in the nest that I saw, when God spoke to me in my military quarters several years before I met my mentor. Only one flew before the other. She is a part of this new family of mine. She is my sister! There was never a negative thought concerning her in my mind. Only a few positive words that she had spoken to me in short conversations to give me assurance. I even understood the *thorns in her nest.* Those same thorns were still there and they had become mine.

As I was certainly lost for words, I felt the intensity of demonic activity increase in the atmosphere... **"Crucify her, crucify her",** they screamed. **"Give us Barrabus, but crucify her"!** Though broken and wounded, with the arrows stuck in my heart, this, too, I *willingly forgave.*

There was one thing that my enemies (Satan and his imps) had forgotten. God himself had anointed me with the costly perfume of His Spirit when he had prepared me for burial. Furthermore, I had died before they killed me. They did not take my life. I gave it when we were all at the funeral of my flesh a few months prior.

One prophet had recently told me in a service, "God is about to induce your labor." I laughed sarcastically, because I knew that it meant "P" to the **"fourth"** power, *"Pregnant, Pain, Pressure, and Push"!* This is every woman's battle.

DAY OF DEATH

At the time that I walked in deep hatred for the women that shared *the nest* with me, they were like tiny bugs that crawled around and bugged me.

One weekend while seeking the Lord, He told me that I needed to die to myself, and forgive. He gave me the plan and obituary for the funeral of my flesh. I personally got up that Sunday morning and apologized to all of the women. The Lord had me to invite the whole congregation to this spiritual funeral. I shared the vision of my spiritual funeral with them. I had seen myself in a spiritual casket dying to my flesh. I shared it with tears of brokenness.

At the end of the service my pastor "The Eagle Called, Dad" told every woman to give me a hug. I tell you those were the most anointed hugs that I had ever encountered. Each hug seemed to destroy a particular yoke of bondage, as the shells would fall off. This bird was coming forth. Those shells are presently there in the nest. They represent my past.

I had never felt so much love for women, as I did on that day. The thing that hurt you will sometimes be the very thing that heals you. Doctors fight disease with disease, to get your system immune to the infection. I allowed the rejection that came from a few, cause me to hate the whole portion of that body. My healing began when the ones I hated – I forgave. (My healing was complete when I got to the root) Even the few that rejected me hugged me. That was the dose that healed me the most.

Thorns In My Nest

THE BONA FIDE "LIFELINE"

After the encounter with the women, my children's personal life at home was not even connected to this world of abandonment. They continued their daily laughing as if nothing had happened.

Deep within me, I was so dismantled that I could not concentrate on one thing for one minute. Nights and days were the loneliest ever. Even the divorce that I had gone through did not affect me to this magnitude. This was a deeper separation because this was the "family of God."

The cord was broken, not cut. (To cut the cord leaves a sense of peace. To break the cord leaves pain to everyone involved).

My family in the nest, were the ones that would say to me, "We are in covenant". They would promise me their loyalty and commitment to our relationship. They would stand in public places, like hotels and restaurants and tell me that I was family. Some even said, "Call me anytime." This day, I felt that I was in the family but, only as the newest kid on the block, and the blackest sheep of the fold, separated and left alone.

The eagle called "Mom" loved me no matter what. Even though, words from the spirit of Jezebel revealed something different. The covenant was so strong with Mom that every evil

106

thought that I would have was conquered with a powerful Word in my spirit.

I loved her with a pure love that was ordained by God. I had to be careful with what I allowed myself to listen to concerning her. Focusing was a battle for me. Besides looking to Jesus for strength to remain in the nest, I saw before me the covenant and love that I had for her.

My cord was attached to her. That cord was the lifeline that God had created for a "temporary" connection. When I left the nest the enemy "broke" the cord, *but he could not break the blood. Our relationship was* connected by the cord, but ordained by the blood. Cords dry up and fall off- *The Blood Keeps On Flowing.*

Furthermore, God uses people in our lives to nurture us for a season, but he never wants us to depend on them. He doesn't want them to become a crutch, in our faith walk with Him. Neither does He want us to look for them to do, what He wants to do in us and through us. The whole point in mentoring is to teach others to have faith in God, not in man. I can literally hear God say, "**From man to Me.**" This is the bona fide lifeline. This is the real deal - **To have faith in God, the Father.**

THORNS IN MY NEST

As I ventured off for the next few weeks, I found myself moving. I moved from the house that I had gotten to make more room for my friend. I even moved in my mind as I dealt with many emotions and torments. Finally, I moved in a spiritual sense... to a place called *hell.*

My bed was made of thorns..." *Thorns In My Nest*". These thorns were the many painful things that hurt in *the nest*. The thorns felt like sharp blades that would cut into me every so often.

I was so distressed and torn apart. I had a mental breakdown. I literally lost my mind. I was unable to make reasonable decisions. (It was only by the Grace of God that I landed in my husband's hands. He was a ram in the bush). It was as though even the shells had come back to engulf and trap me again.

The rejections, the lies, the loneliness, the betrayals, the misunderstandings, the disappointments, the ugliness, the low self-esteem, the fear of failure, they were all thorns in my nest.

People that hurt me were like thorns. People that looked for my downfall were like thorns. I was simply surrounded by thorns. My nest was made up of them.

Darkness was my address. My house was webbed with confusion. A confusion that only got worse if I tried to figure it out. It was like trying to pull a web apart, only to find it sticking and knotting together with no true place to start at. (Sounds like a Jezebel spirit to me!)

There was a stone placed at the wall of my heart, which was the door of my house, (that I myself could not roll away). I was barricaded by grief. I could not get out and no one could get in. Angels of death and darkness guarded it day and night.

"Where was Mom?" I cried! Where was Dad? I had no home. I was a homeless bastard child! That's the way I felt. I did not feel grown, when I left. I felt hurt.

I became a spiritual hoodlum, with nowhere to go. I hung out on the street corners of darkness. I stuck people up in the spirit by robbing them of their joy. I was doing drive-bys in my mind, killing the saints with my thoughts. I was back "*in the hood*" where I was "*before the nest.*"

At one point I was numb. I had no emotion, no pain, no hurt, no anointing (so it seemed). I was not, because I was in a dead state of mind. By this time, I wished that I could at least feel the pain. I wanted to feel something. If I could have just felt something, then, I "thought," I would be able to deal with it.

When all my feelings were dead, my only reliance was my knowing. I knew God was real, though I could not express it. I knew that He had called me, though I could not respond. I knew that He loved me, though I could not feel it.

My knowing, at this time, was deeper than any feeling. My knowing was my way out. It was a "*Key.*" If He were to show up, I'd recognize Him because of what I knew. I knew Him. I knew His

Word. Knowledge is powerful, but heartfelt knowledge is explosive. It is "rhema", and it is *life*. *Do You Know Him?*

The grip that the enemy had on my mind was like a torture that I had never experienced. He cuffed my head and squeezed it with great pressure. I had no control over my thought life as my very thoughts tormented me, bringing back memories that left me with no sense of direction. (The spirit of Jezebel had taken over!)

I regressed backward to every hurt in my life, including pain from my high school days when my mother slapped me for crying over a boy. She did not understand that I had a deep soul-tie. The pain that I had left *"in the hood"*, resurfaced with power. I got mad at the boy again. Thought after thought reminded me of *the nest.*

The smiles that I could once use to cover my disappointments had departed. The facade was lifting from my face. The ugly roots were hanging out. I snapped at every human that looked like they wanted to make me mad.

Even in the grocery stores I was evil. I found a reason to hate nice people. To me everyone was out to get me. Now, I wanted to hurt every body. I wanted to brutally beat someone with great pleasure. *Hurting people, hurt people.*

Ninety percent of the time, I was quiet. But it was a quiet rage. An inner turmoil was going on. I did not call anyone in *the nest* to give an explanation of what was going on. I, myself, could not understand any of it. It was very unnatural for me to be quiet most of the time. I am gifted to talk to people.

I talked to one sister, but she too was in the "belly of the fish", with seaweed wrapped around her head. Just like Jonah (Jonah 1:17), God had prepared a great fish to swallow us. We were both waiting to be spit out.

"The waters compassed me about, even to the soul: the depth closed me round about, the weeds were wrapped about my head." (Jonah 2:5)

When I did feel some pain, it was a hurt that was so deep that it cut to the core.

I wanted to break, but I had no access to the hammer-*the Word of God*. Even when I tried to read the Word, there was no release. My Bible became quite dusty, as it lay coupled with other books. For one whole year, I read not one page. However, the Word of God was packed in my spirit-*deep within me*. It was locked away in my spirit. I just wanted a key.

My eyes had run to the point that the waters were gone. Crying was not easy and this made it worse. Though I sowed in tears, I was waiting to reap in joy. Every pain, rejection and hurt was simply a reminder of the wounds that Christ received on the cross for me. It reminds me of His blood that He shed for my healing. It also reminds me of "*the battle*". This battle was the one that Jesus fought in hell (the battle in my mind in the place of the skull-Golgotha). I myself was on this same course, so it seemed. I walked through hell only viewing the ugly face of bitterness, unforgiveness and absolute anger. Eventually, in a hotel in Cold Water, Michigan, I came across the words "solitude and listen". These two words would soon be keys to my deliverance. In the quietness of the morning, I heard the Lord speak in a still small voice-"*Listen in Solitude, Just Listen*".

I had so much bitterness in my heart that it felt as if my flesh was slowly melting away and I would soon cease to be. I wanted to forgive but I hated to the point of murdering. Church people were a nuisance in my sight. Anybody talking about church was simply on my hit list. As far as I was concerned, they were fake and phony. Prophecy, anointing, calling, purpose, destiny, and chosen vessel were words that I despised. I hated talking about eagles. My vision was dead. It was hard to think that God was on my side. If so, "Why did He allow this to happen?" I'd ask. After a large truck with eighteen wheels ran me off of the highway, I knew that it was judgment day for me. I thought that God was going to allow the devil to kill me one way or another. In the night, the torment deepened as I lay on my pillow.

Hell had chambers that housed many different spirits. It was an orderly place. Each spirit knew when it was his time to enter and manifest. It was an organized place filled with many different ranks of demons. The stronger demons, such as fear, seemed to open doors for lower ranking ones. I hated this place. If only I could have fought when I wanted to. I wanted to fight, but it seemed to have been an appointed time for my resurrection. I couldn't pray it up and I couldn't praise it up. I could only *"Wait it out"*. *Time was an appointment.* Until then, I was buried in a place called *hell,* waiting for the *"key"* to unlock death and step into life! My *"Key"* came when the Housekeeper knocked at my door. By this time I'd spent *"three days in the belly of hell."*

"It is good for me that I have been afflicted; that I might learn thy statutes." Psalms 119:71

Except a seed first fall to the ground and die, it cannot reproduce. Even your vision must DIE in order to LIVE.
1Corinthians 15:36

SPIRITUALLY SPEAKING...

I DIED
THE NEST DIED
THE MENTORS DIED
THE VISION DIED
THE SPIRITUAL FAMILY DIED

DEATH WAS INEVITABLE, IF I WAS TO LIVE!!!

I ENDURED MY CROSS!

I know you may say, "God how can I rest my head on these thorns?" Ask Jesus what did he do in Gethsemane? He died before he actually died. He drank the cup of suffering. Dead things don't move. God wants to use you but you need to die to yourself. Death is inevitable if you want his resurrected life and power in your ministry, family and church.

Some of you are trying to flee the nest because the going is rough. Go through! Go through to the other side of your cross. Though, I left the nest fifteen months too soon, I still had to endure my cross. I died where I was. Death met me there. However, I picked up a few battles that I could have avoided. Some of those battles I am still fighting by faith.

If you endure hardness as a good soldier, God will cause your *nest of thorns* to be turned over for a *crown of life*. The "Key" is to endure. *God has given you an anointing to endure.*

It is time that you plan the funeral of your flesh by way of crucifixion. As I remembered my death, this is what came to mind...

Jesus read my eulogy. It read:

In Memory Of   **KEEBEE HARDAWAY**
Born In Sin...............June 26, 1963   Reborn.............. February 1, 1982
Died To Herself...................1995   Resurrected..........after three days in hell

---

In the year that she saw the Lord, He was high and lifted up and His train filled the temple of her heart.   She is known and loved by the God of her salvation, Jesus Christ. She is accepted by the beloved-God. It no longer matters what people think about her because she is wonderfully and beautifully made. God is her Maker and her Lover. She departed the carnal life of walking in the flesh by forgiving others and leaving to mourn, many worries, rejections and miseries, and a great host of other demonic forces that tormented her daily. The miseries will miss her because they loved her company. Rejections caused her to have low self-esteem. Deception her closest friend will miss her dearly.

She also leaves to mourn a host of demons that enjoyed when she operated in her flesh. Oh! She will be greatly missed in her flesh. Though she is absent from walking in the flesh, she will no longer mind the things of the flesh. She understood to be carnally minded was death; but to be spiritually minded is life and peace. In her flesh she could not please her God. Because Christ is in her, her body is dead because of sin; but the Spirit in her is life because of righteousness. NOW THAT SHE"S LED BY THE SPIRIT OF GOD, SHE IS A SON OF GOD.

Her life in the spirit will leave a legacy to her children and her children's children. Her name will be well known in the kingdom of Satan. She will Be a Key that will unlock and set the captives free. She will no longer take the Harder Way out. Key-Be will now Be a Key. She shall take the King's Way.

Her King, "Jesus", the Lord of her life is the Master Key and she shall be a copy of Him. Her life SHALL be a Key that will "Be" and exist in this earth realm because the Lord hath anointed her to preach good tidings unto the meek; He hath sent her to bind up the brokenhearted, to proclaim liberty to the captives, and the opening of the prison to them that are bound.

Launch Out and Explore Death!

It is very well possible to live a defeated Christian life. I lived this way saved and all for many years until I decided to die to myself, no matter what the cost. During my funeral, I had a Gethsemane experience.

As I stood in the presence of this crowd, I remembered my death. I remembered the obituary that I saw. I remembered not moving. There was a stillness that left me standing in the Presence of the Lord as I had an awesome vision of myself dying to myself. My funeral was packed with witnesses that were used to seeing me move. All of a sudden I died that He may live. Launch out and stop living a defeated Christian life! DIE!

All Negatives Need Exposure

While in *the nest*, I would take my eyes off of God and look at people and situations. I seemed to lose focus of what God was really doing. God did not want me to be concerned about the people and situations. He wanted me to stay focused. Before vision is fulfilled, focus is adjusted. (In some cases it is shifted if you are trying to focus on the wrong thing.) Stay focused and see the big picture. Focus is activated before the picture is taken.

Blind men can't take pictures. Get your vision clear. I had many negatives and many issues. My whole past was a negative. My family was a negative in a dysfunctional way. My life was a negative. All the negatives that the enemy had gathered against me would soon be developed in the darkroom of hell in the waters of the true and living God, to form a beautiful picture. The darkroom is set up to expose all of your negatives. Exposure is the first step to fulfillment. The colors in negatives are always the opposite of what the picture really is, that's why it needs exposure.

Being opposite means having opposition. It may be dark, but God's going to bring you out. You fight off opposing forces in the darkroom of hell where the keys are stripped from the enemies of your faith. You have got to go to hell!

God's vision is picture perfect. He always starts with a negative, in order to bring you into the picture. Negatives can always be reproduced over and over and over again. If you fail, He'll do it again. It's not over until God says its over. *Now smile while God snaps your shot!*

From Man To "Me"

Writing this book has been strictly out of my experience. I have written the contents, as I have learned. This has to be the most important section of this book, as far as I am concerned. The whole process of the nest was to get me to this point.

In the past God allowed my mentors to be present for a certain period in my life. Just as children need parental guidance until a certain age, so did I, in a spiritual sense. They will always be my parents, and I will always honor them. However, it was now time for me to move out and try my wings in a more mature way. God used man, but now God wants to be Himself in me. He doesn't want other peoples standards of success to influence my destiny. Neither does He want me to base my success on how others around me have succeeded. He has set standards for my life and He wants to be at the wheel to control the steering. When you are used to having Mom and Dad to bell you out of danger zones, it can create a crutch in your faith walk with God. It can create a co-dependency.

One thing is for certain, "You can not marry your mama and your daddy." (This is something that one of my covenant sisters told me.) And if you are to marry, you must leave in order to cleave.

God wanted me all to Himself. If I had not allowed Him to properly cut the attachment to my spiritual parents, faith according to the Word of God would not have been exercised in my life.

Leaving and cleaving takes faith. Faith is the only way to please God. It is impossible to please Him without it. Good parents will let you go when it's time to move out.

My greatest fear has always been that I would be left alone or abandoned. Trusting God totally, with no human interference was new heights for me. I found out that the same God that was there for Elijah was the same God that showed up for Elisha. He was also the God of Abraham, Isaac and Jacob. I trust Him and I trust His covenant plan for my life.

Now that God has broken the soul-tie and co-dependent behavior off of my life, I can trust Him totally. I never wanted to be left alone. Furthermore, I found out that the type of anointing that God has placed on my life requires that I spend most of my time alone with Him and, not people. We all need somebody from time to time for Godly counsel. However, the enemy tried to destroy me with the element that I needed the most in my life "The ability to walk alone." He wanted to destroy me with the thing that I was anointed to do. "Get alone in His presence."

There is one thing that the Lord revealed to me after I switched, from man to Him. It is impossible for me to be left alone. I can't be left alone because I am now with the one who will never leave me nor forsake me. He is omni-present (everywhere at once). Man may leave me, but God can't leave me. I will never be the same after understanding and knowing this.

I am no longer abandoned or rejected because my faith is now in the right place-In God. I made the shift in my focus from man to God. Jesus is the object of my faith. You too need to make the shift.

7

THE FALL OF MAN CALLED, "ME"

"Now the serpent was more subtil than any beast of the field which the Lord God had made. And he said unto the woman, yea, hath God said, Ye shall not eat of every tree of the garden? And the woman said unto the serpent, we may eat of the fruit of the trees of the garden: but the fruit of the tree which is in the midst of the garden, God hath said, ye shall not eat of it, neither shall ye touch it, lest ye die. And the serpent said unto the woman, ye shall NOT SURELY die."

Genesis 3:1-4

 123

CHAPTER SEVEN

The Fall Of Man Called, "Me"

In the midst of my nest there went up a mist from the earth, and watered the whole face of the ground (My intercession). And the Lord formed me from the dust and the dirt of that nest (The gossip, rejection, and lies). Then He breathed into my nostrils the breath of life (His spirit upon me); and I became a living soul. This was the spiritual creation of the eagle that occupied that nest, *myself* as viewed in my heart.

Out of the ground the Lord God made every tree grow that was pleasant to the sight, and good for food. The tree of life grew in the midst of the garden (My nest), and the tree of knowledge of good and evil. A river was there to water the garden (My worship experience). The Lord God took me and put me into the garden to dress it and to keep it (My obedience). This garden was the environment in which I resided. And the Lord God commanded me, saying, "Of every tree of the garden thou may eat: but, the tree of the knowledge of good and evil thou shalt not eat of it

(Temptations): for in the day that thou eatest thereof thou shalt *surely* die." This was the forbidden fruit.

A forbidden fruit in today's terms could be anything that God has told us not to touch such as, adultery, fornication, lying, murdering, etc. What is your forbidden fruit? What is it that you struggle with? What is it that you are trying to force into the will of God? We need to know our boundaries and limitations. I once saw a sign that read, "*Forbidden fruits create many jams*". Jams can be some sticky situations. I knew this all too well.

In my nest, there stood a serpent more subtil than any beast of that field. He laid in wait for the very moment that I was at my *weakest*. I had managed to avoid him up to the point that Judas kissed me. I struggled the tenure of my stay in the nest with this serpent. He was the most hideous animal that I had ever known. He was cunning and crafty. Many times he would say to me, "Your mother the eagle doesn't really love you." That's the devil's favorite line when you walk in a spirit of rejection. He would fight the relationship that God had so divinely connected. I struggled with this serpent.

In the nest I did not know his name but, as I jumped onto the branch after leaving the nest, God my Great Eagle named Jesus, revealed his name and face to me. His name was *DECEPTION*. He had no one face because he had enough power to be what he wanted to at that moment to deceive me. (A spirit of deception has many faces). Deception approached me many times. I can remember The Eagle called "Mom" had laid her claws upon my head and rebuked Deception. She saw his face before I did. Of course, I was young and could barely see. I had the eye of an eaglet while she had the eye of an eagle.

Her spiritual head was as white as snow because she had reached the age of maturity. I was still a black greyish color (not too attractive to look upon). It took time and years and some experience for the white to come. The white head of that eagle to me represented purity and maturity. The white head made that eagle to look bald and it gave it great beauty. (For the Saint of God that is the Beauty of Holiness).

I thought that I had overcome the spirit of deception. The bible says that a man ought not think more highly of himself than he should (Galatians 6:3). When I received my kiss from Judas, my enemy called Deception was there by my side. I did not struggle with him this time. I was *too* weak to fight. I was dying from a broken cord. I can remember the weakness that I felt in basic training when I was hungry and weak from marching in the heat all day. This is the same feeling that I had in a spiritual sense. The heat was on and I was weary, weak and worn, as the old folks would say. Desperately wanting food for my spirit, I felt a faint coming on (that is a spiritual faint). I could do nothing on my own, it seemed, but fail, and that I did.

The thing that I had held on to up to that point, I let it go. I ate the forbidden fruit of fornication. Even though, I had been married before and had two natural born children from that union, God told me that he had restored to me (in the realm of the spirit) my God given purity and virtue. I was faithful to hold up to this for a number of years without giving in to my flesh. I truly felt in control and delivered. But, when the storm came, I tore away from my apostolic parents when trouble arrived. When rejection came in, I gave myself to a man. I had touched "*the forbidden thing*" and was caught in a jam. I had a great fall. This was very difficult for me, due to the fact that I had held a standard. Even though this all happened before I entered the ministry, it still had a great effect on me.

Let's Get Down To Earth, Before We Get To Heaven

Years ago before allowing God to do a work in me, I can recall the times that I thought that I would find true love according to what I offered men in the flesh. This was my place of struggle. As men and women, we do not always stop to think about the consequences that we might suffer, as a result of the decisions that we make. Because we do not know what a real man and a real woman are, we choose mates according to what we know through experience and have been taught through observation. We do all that we know to do, which means that we do not know enough. Our ignorance leads us to death. Many times we find ourselves in so much pain and rejection that, when a man or woman shows us a little attention, we get caught up in it and mistaken it for love. This can leave some devastating emotional, physical and sexual soul ties.

When rejection has you seeking for love in all the wrong places, you find yourself jumping in and out of beds with every person that comes your way. When it is all over, your guilt is so strong and intense that you go into a state of deep depression and self-hatred. You ask yourself, "Why am I doing this?" You come out feeling dirty and cheap. Your words of negativity become self-fulfilling prophecies.

As for women, after the man has placed his claws into her and he is done with her, it kills her self-esteem. Most people want someone to want them for who they really are. The problem is, they don't know who they are. On the inside, they know that there is more to them than they are manifesting. That small inside voice always says, "you are worth more", but for some reason that worth is hard to pinpoint.

Relationships can be addictive, not so much sexually, but the companionship part of it. It can lead to the hope that someone will receive you and even ask you for marriage. Don't sell yourself *like* that of a whore. (Men that lay with many women are whores as well. It is a spirit of whoredom.) The bible calls a whore a harlot, that is another term used for prostitute).

Don't keep having baby after baby, abortion after abortion, and relationship after relationship. It doesn't take long to find out if someone is empty of character and substance, and lack responsibility. Remember, that birds of a feather, they all flock together.

Are you an eagle or are you a chicken? If you are an eagle, then why are you flocking with a chicken? If he or she doesn't pay their bills, they are chickens. They will gobble you up. If he or she doesn't pay child support, they are chickens. If he or she doesn't love and serve God with all their heart, mind and soul, *they are chickens.* They reverentially fear and worship other things and people, but not God. *Leave them alone!* You are attracted to your kind. If you are choosing empty men and women, it is probably because you are empty too? *Change your company, flock with the eagles. Eagles Soar!* Bad company corrupts good character. You choose empty men because you are an empty woman (the same goes for you men). You are looking for substance, but true substance is found in Jesus. Realistically, you don't need a mate. You need Jesus.

It amazes me how women will change their bodies to please a man. They will cut on it, add to it, neglect it by throwing up (bulimia), not feed it at all (anorexia), etc. You think you're too fat or too skinny, too tall or too small (low self-esteem). We lack that validation many times due to our lack of being fathered. It is the father that does the validating of the children. *Men bless your seed.*

If we have a wayward or wild mother that makes an impact on us as well. Women leave their children quicker than ever, for drugs and relationships. Children need to be nurtured in the admonition of the Lord. Women are great nurturers when they walk in purpose.

Sin has consequences. Some men (and women) are physically present but not actively involved in their children's lives. That makes them emotionally or spiritually absent (MIA or missing in action). Some are not there at all (just gone AWOL, absent without leave). With a nonchalant attitude, they say, "See Ya!"

No matter what you feel about this subject, it is not my opinion it is the infallible word of God. Please talk it out with Jesus if you disagree. I say this in much love. You must see the plan and vision for the total family of God. It starts with you as an individual. Families are made up of individuals. Communities are made up of families. *Families should go to church together.* States are made up of communities, and so on. God is interested in family. God wanted a family when he created man. He has *"the original"* idea of family. Not Adam and Steve, but Adam and Eve. He also had a man in place when the children were born. Adam and Eve were husband and wife. Anything other than that plan reaps consequences to come in subsequent generations.

Most likely, if you don't agree with that you are probably doing the opposite of it. It is very selfish to not consider your future offspring when you plan to create your *own* idea of family. This is a sin of omission. When you pass over truth or neglect it, not insert it, or mention it, then you are omitting it.

Many of our children are not taught the bible way, which happens to be the way of truth. Therefore, our sons grow up not having the blueprint for family. Our daughters grow up not knowing how to recognize a man and lack the knowledge of real womanhood. For a lack of knowledge our children are perishing in the form of generational curses instead of generational blessings. They repeat what they are taught or what they learn through observation within their environment *(wrong thought patterns based upon what they perceived as family)*. I had to get a hold of this truth, myself.

I would say that my family was totally dysfunctional. I started out walking in a generational curse. I did many terrible things. Through much heart felt and fervent prayer, knowledge of the word of God and commitment to my God, the curse has been broken. I am free. My children are free. My offspring are free. Even this book and the future books that I am presently writing will bless my offspring. *This is my legacy for my children's children.*

Here's something to think about for the women. When "you allow" men to use your body, and they reject you, your self worth gets shot. You simply have no self-esteem left. For the moment that you were giving in, all you could think about was, "Well it feels good right now and he's giving me attention", so you sell yourself cheap.

My sister, sister, you are worth more than what a million dollars can buy. You are not measured by money. You are measured by the fiber of God's character that dwells in you. Character cannot be brought with a buck or two. It is developed in the obscurity of the smallest trials of life. You are being *"made"* whole in your soul, transformed and renewed in your mind. However, you are already wonderfully and beautifully made in your spirit. *You are beautiful!*

If you are not careful, rejection will show up in some ugly ways, including a need to have somebody, no matter how bad they are and how awful they treat you. Don't except anything as a man or a woman. When you have a need to be loved, it is easy to lower your standards. Rejection will cause you to lower your standards. I am reminded of a time that I was so tired of waiting on Boaz to show up that I got all excited when a counterfeit of a man brought me an ironing board. It made me feel so special because I was in such a desperate and rejected state. It was the lowest that I had gone for a man. It was not hard for me to buy my own ironing board. I was just lonely and that attention almost made me give in to someone who didn't even buy shoes for his own children.

Learn to recognize the causes of rejection as well as the manifestations of them. That spirit shows up in many different ways and is one of the root causes to most social and behavioral problems. It can manifest itself in aggressive attitudes such as swearing, fighting, argumentativeness, and over achievement to try to prove yourself to others, for acceptance. It will make you disrespect the position of manhood or womanhood. It can manifest itself in low self-image, and fear of failure or fear of people. Many of our rejections go back to our childhood. Rejection is a poisonous purpose killer.

Relationships, "just for the moment", have an affect on women in different ways than men. It directly destroys them. It also destroys men in a slow, ugly way. The enemy lies to men and sends them off walking in a false sense of manhood. He endows them and puffs them up with pride. *My brother, this one is for you.* Any man that thinks what is in his pants makes him who he is, he is certainly empty and void and full of "puff" (air). The enemy tends to build men up to make them think that is what manhood is all about. If this is your thinking, you are lost and need to meet the real man Jesus to understand true manhood and Godly character. I am not beating on men. I am just exposing the devil.

Real men have Godly substance. They are full of "*God Stuff*". God is training up some great Men of God that will not seek to use and abuse the good thing that God will cause them to find. There is a diamond in the rough being made for you. You need to have substance (God stuff) to pour into her and cover her when she's presented to you. *Adam Where Are You?* A real man of God will enhance his wife's purpose in God.

Women, if you want your Boaz to find you, you must prepare yourself by beautifying your spirit with the word of God, then God can present you to the man. Eve was fully formed and made whole before she was presented. Some of you are too messed up for the presentation. Let God finish the work in you. Make Godly decisions that come from a good conscience. The conscience is darkened when the light of the word is not present. Why would God tell you that He's going to send you a good man if he is not going to make you a *"good woman"*? *You need some "God Stuff" too! You need to learn how to respect yourself.*

People will treat you the way you treat yourself. If you behave like a whore, men will treat you that way. If you dress like one, they will dress you that way. If you lack Godly character, you are the enemy of yourself. Charity begins at home. Love God, so that you can love you and ultimately love others. A real woman of God will enhance the purpose of her Boaz.

My present husband, who is a natural born African from Nigeria, was taught manhood and leadership as a part of his culture. Believe it or not, this *does not* necessarily make Africans real men. A real man is "A real man", because of his Godly character. Having strong cultural teaching without God's Word would only make them controlling and arrogant. But, the Word of God balances everything a particular culture teaches.

The Word lets us know what to hold on to and what to throw out. Let God develop you into the man or woman that he has called you to be. Forget the moments of pleasure that only leave you empty and lonely. You may be walking alone, but you do not have to be lonely. Alone is, "All one". It gives the idea of singleness that indicates wholeness. Wholeness is when you are lined up and prospering spirit, soul and body. God said, "I will never leave you nor forsake you". God is with you. Please him, and I guarantee you that he will please you. He does not please you, because you please him. He will please you because He's God, He is sovereign and He got it that way. If you don't please him, certainly you won't be pleased. Give Him moments of pleasure and intimacy. Let him woo you in the depth of your heart. You will never go back. Try Christ, you will see a real man!!! He will always be a Man of His Word. He won't leave you comfortless.

"Even the youths shall faint and be weary, and the young men shall utterly fall: but they that wait upon the Lord shall renew their strength; they shall mount up with wings as eagles; they shall run, and not be weary; and they shall walk, and not faint." (Isaiah 40:30-31)

8

DON'T KILL THE BABY!

"And the Lord God formed man of the dust of the ground, and breathed into his nostrils the breath of life; and man became a living soul."

Genesis 2:7

CHAPTER EIGHT

Don't Kill The Baby

After eating the forbidden fruit of fornication, weeks later, to my surprise, there growing in my womb was an unborn child. The pregnancy added more fuel to my ongoing fire. Along with being pregnant I was sick to the point that I was bed ridden. It was a physical struggle. I eventually had my god-sister Audrey help me after I confided in her that I was pregnant.

Audrey had been in the nest awhile. I thought she would be gone from the nest by this time, but she could not seem to break out of the shell of her past. Therefore, she was like a *"holdover"* (a military term used to describe a person that is in basic training longer than the original plan allows.) She used to tell everyone, *"Beware of the dream-stealers"*. That was her message. Her past always seemed to steal her dream. I thank God now she's dreaming again. She stood by me in the subsequent days...and so goes the saying, "A friend in need is a friend indeed". For this I am grateful.

Upon finding out that I was expecting, my failure deepened. I wanted to hide because of shame. *Deception said, "Kill it! Kill that baby!"* It opened the door for a *murdering spirit* in which I had been delivered from. (Abortion was easy for me, because I had done it before.) In the middle of my bed I lay there while a spirit of murder had crept in. Suicide was easy and relieving, so I thought. I just could not go out like that. Although at times, it seemed as if death had to be better than this loneliness and grief that I was experiencing.

As I lay in my bed, if felt as if the walls of my room began to come in as if to squeeze me. I was running out of breath. I had a feeling of deep suffocation. My house was dirty from one end to the other. This was totally out of character for me. I cared about nothing. I could not scream or cry aloud but the tears were heavy.

Underneath my voice, I heard a small sound that said, "*JESUS*". Immediately there was a "*MERCY*" ring on my telephone and I found enough strength to answer it. On the other line was a woman that I used to go and get out of the crack houses. I had taught her how to pray. We used to get in my housing project (in the nest) and call on the name of the Lord almost daily. We laid hands on the drug addicts and dealers together. We were serious about our mission to minister to those around us. I loved her as my *"dearest"* sister. Not many ever believed she would ever be anything in God. But, I saw the greatest jewel. I saw her in the dirtiest state and I saw her in the cleanest state, for she struggled deeply with drugs, herself. I never gave up on her even though, at times I wanted to beat her upside the walls. *She's my sister!*

When she walked in the things of God she had a settlement within her that was deep. Her very temperament demanded that people around her respect her. She had within her great potential to be a "Woman of God". That is what she is now. During that time she walked in a very immature but holy correction and reproofing anointing.

I regret not paying more attention to our relationship as covenant sisters, when I somehow found myself busy with another friend. *I cut the cord with her and it felt like I broke the blood.* This I strongly regret, but with much relief in my heart I say, "*I'm sorry.*" It wasn't intentional but it was one of those things that I know hurt her. God revealed that to me when he delivered me.

When I picked up the phone, the woman said, "Sis Keebee what is going on, I feel you." (It was Sis Euna Whitehead, my blood covenant sister). I started crying loud and uncontrollably. She hung up the phone and was at my house in about ten minutes. *What a dedicated friend!* When she walked in, she did not ask any questions and I had not told her anything. She immediately went to battle on my behalf. She began to rebuke the spirit of death, murder and suicide. *She fought for me with her armor. She fought my battle. Again that's the power of covenant.* She said, "I know that you are pregnant, the Lord showed me. **Don't kill the baby**".

On another occasion Sis. Euna called me as I was on my face praying and crying at 8:30 in the morning. I do not answer my phone when I am talking to the Lord, but that day I did. She prophesied every word verbatim that I was praying. She did it with power. I had never heard her under that type of anointing before. It touched me deeply. It was a strategic moment of confirmation and assurance. New hope had come to me. By the way "New Hope" was the name of my home church that I'd left *in the nest*.

As long as I was fellowshipping with my brothers and sisters at New Hope, I had no problem with my sexual desires and need to be loved. They held me together. They gave me strength. I was accountable to them. There was even a small-framed mother that believed in me. She encouraged me daily as we met in prayer. Her name was Mother Lott. Mother Lott had a lot to offer. She herself was a "Big Lot", a fertile land flowing with milk and honey. It was as though her bones were full of the anointing. I loved hanging around that little old lady. She loved every one.

All of the church mothers seemed to help me in one-way or another. I sat very close to them to close out my warfare as I praised God with all of my heart every Sunday, faithfully. This helped me to stay focused. I was hanging out with the "Grand-Mama Eagles" (The mother's of the church). All the saints there were a part of my body. I did finally love them, after the funeral of my flesh, when I died to myself. We sharpened each other. It seemed to me that God had set up a people that wanted purpose and destiny, even though they all had their personal battles.

It is so important that we discern those around us. In the book of John when Jesus met the woman at the well, she did not know who He was. She could not discern Him. Jesus said to her, "*If thou knewest the gift of God, and who it is that saith to thee Give me to drink; thou wouldest have asked of him, and he would have given thee living water*". That's what Sister Euna gave to me that day, "Living Water".

The saints of God are so powerful in each other's life. Just because you don't agree on everything, doesn't mean that a person is not of God. Learn to know those who labor among you. It just might be the person that saves your life.

No Face To Face

"The Word of God is quick, and powerful, and sharper than any two edged sword, piercing even to the dividing asunder of soul and spirit, and of the joints and marrow, and is a discerner of the thoughts and intents of the heart" (*Hebrews 4:12*). In other words, it will cut going in and coming out. It cuts in every direction. God's word cut the enemy's plan, but he also cut into my soul and spirit. It discerned my very thoughts and all of my negatives and divided that which was God from that which was not. I tell you after a kiss from Judas you will have some thoughts. God will cause all within your heart to surface. Those are the things that will go to the cross with you. What is left after the death on your personal cross is what remains for the Master's use. When Jesus was on the cross, I believe that He dealt with all sins of the world, whether in thought or deed (including abortion).

I know many of you have been through many trials and tribulations. There should be a life changing experience as you come out. I tell people when they are in a troubled place or a struggling space, look for the wisdom of God. Wisdom of God is found in the mind of God. The mind of God is the Word of God. His Word is a spiritual weapon. It is the sword of the Spirit. The Word of God will bring liberty and healing.

I never had anyone minister to me in reference to the pain of past abortions that I had. It was one of those personal and secret torments for me. I experienced terrible nightmares, as a result. I can remember one specific nightmare that haunted me. The police showed up at my door to arrest me because they found my aborted baby in the dumpster in my back yard. I was handcuffed and taken to jail. It was so real in my mind. The enemy constantly tormented me about going to hell for murder. I feared hell because of what I had done. The shame of it haunted me.

I cried over what that child would be like, and what he or she would be. Was it a prophet? Was it a doctor? I wanted to know if it was a boy or girl. Many thoughts I struggled with. God wanted to use it to set other women free but I could not talk about it. Now that he's set me free, I must pass on the key. Now take this *Key* "*forgive yourself*? God desires that you be healed totally. The enemy formed the weapon against you, but it shall not prosper. "For we have not an high priest which cannot be touched with the feeling of our infirmities; but was in all points tempted like as we are, yet without sin. Let us therefore come boldly unto the throne of grace that we may obtain mercy, and find grace to help in time of need" (Hebrews 4:15-16.)

"And we know that all things WORK together for good to them that love God, to them who are the called according to HIS purpose." (Romans 8:28)

No matter where you've been or where you've come from it will *work!* Tell the Lord right now to just "*work it!*"

Life in the womb is a creation done by God alone. I have seen man place a baby in the womb and attempt to clone a man. However, I have not ever seen him create a sperm. God alone is the Creator of the seed. If you are pregnant out of wedlock and you are contemplating having an abortion, "***Don't kill that baby***". Break that spirit of rejection from the womb. Stop killing purpose! Some of us abort spiritually and reject the purpose of God in us. We have a fear of being responsible and accountable. To much is given, much is required. ***Don't Kill Your Baby!*** Had I continued on in a spirit of rejection, I would have aborted this book (My baby!) Think about it.

Those of you with physical children in your womb need to understand that that baby is there for a reason. Men don't usually share the pain of abortion with the woman. However, if you paid for, agreed with or encouraged the abortion, you need to repent and ask for forgiveness yourself *(it was done with blood money)*. If you are struggling with your choice, forgive yourself as well.

If you are a *dead-beat dad or mom*, you have also aborted those children in your life in an immoral and mental way. Repent! Get some life in your step and take care of your children. Your beat is dead because they don't hear you stepping around in their lives. They need your step, they need your heart, they need your money, and they need your attention. They also need you at the football game. They need a physical "you". Your "emotional abortion" is worse because you have *"No Face To Face"* with your children and they have a face. Face your responsibilities.

Fornication is the sin, but the baby is not. Adultery is a sin, but the child is not. Life is precious. When you honor life, you honor God. God is life. My greatest test ever, came to me when I became pregnant out of wedlock. It was a test for my honor of life. It was a test to see if I was truly delivered from that murdering demon that once led my life. I had to break through all the shame, pain and pride and face people that looked up to me. I had to swallow it all. I was not suffering because of righteousness I was suffering because I sinned. When I was suffering from the kiss of Judas, it was for righteousness sake. The sin from the pregnancy was fornication, but the baby was life created by God.

To this day, this child is so beautiful in spirit. She is extremely brilliant academically and very obedient. She is so honest that she cried when she found a dime in a department store because she thought she was stealing. I had to get the cashier to accept it from her and then the cashier paid her the dime for being honest. *My baby is already a blessing.* She possesses a particular key in her character that is needed in the church-*Integrity*. What a joy that brings to my heart!

Ask the Lord to forgive you for your sins and thank the Lord for the life that is within you. *God is going to use that child.*

"My God, in the name of Jesus Christ, I speak to the forces of darkness that have come to steal the vision of your people. I command all of hell's angels to be bound, and I loose the Angels of God to carry out the mission. As it is done in heaven, let the Holy Ghost —work it here on earth!!!" I pray for every woman that has had an abortion, and every man that has agreed with It, and every person that has supported it. Let them face the face of the pain of the abortion. I pray for your mercy to cover them. I bind every evil spirit that will torment them in their sleep or otherwise. Let your love come over them. Let each one experience your forgiveness and love.

Even though there's "No Face To Face" with that child, you must loose that pain and let it go. Now forgive yourself!

NO FACE TO FACE

When I look at your face, I can't see who you are,
But you're in my mind, and felt in my heart.
I can see your little toes, and feel your small hands,
I regret the day, I gave you no chance.
You couldn't make a choice, and had no known voice,
Though your destiny is great, cause you're now with the Lord.

When I look at your face, there's a blank on the page,
And a thought in my mind that says that you're dead;
But wrong are my thoughts, when I look at the plan,
Somehow I know that you're in His hands.
No face to face! When I think of your being,
All I can do is trust that you're with him;
I'm sorry for stopping, and cutting you off,
But by it I can somehow, give others a new start.

It was in the hood, that you ceased not to be,
On this earth as we know it,
when you were forced out of me;
Though there's no face, to fill up this space,
I know that you live in a wonderful place.
Out of your death, without a doubt
God will use it to bring others out.
For the torment I suffered, as I went off to sleep,
In the dumpster they found you, and arrested me.

I was handcuffed and taken, to a literal jail,
For killing my baby, "MY GOD THAT WAS HELL."
No more! IN MY MIND, SHALL I SUFFER THIS PAIN,
I FORGIVE MYSELF now, "CAUSE Jesus has paid."
He paid a great price that I might be free,
My baby, my child, "FREE, YES THAT'S ME!"
With time on my hand, and none left for you,
I promise you son...daughter whoever you are,
I will meet you!
MOMMY

"Not by works of righteousness which we have done, but according to his mercy he saved us, by the washing of regeneration, and renewing of the Holy Ghost." (Titus 3:5)

Just as Mercy and Grace have been the faithful angels of my life, God will hold back all hell to bring His Word to past in your life. God has a plan for you. It doesn't matter what you've done. You don't have to have a bad past to be used by God. But for some of us, it's been just that. For those who think that their lives are too cluttered with past sins and negative experiences...*God loves you too!!!*

God is interested in a repentive heart that loves Him. Let God break you, so that you can come forth in contrition. Though the shame of your sin is great, let God remove it with His Word. God has never thrown my past sins in my face, only I have (as well as others.)

We can sometimes be our own and greatest enemy because of the shame that we suffer from our bad choices. Let God remove the shame and bring in the beauty of your face. He will shine His light on you, after He's cleaned you up.

God is not interested in beating you about your failures. That's a part of human error. Your greatest failure is God's greatest opportunity to give you success. Failure simply shows us how much we need God to succeed. *"No matter what the devil has spoken in your ear, it's not over until God says it's over".*

"Comfort ye, comfort ye my people, saith your God. Speak ye comfortably to Jerusalem, and cry unto her, that her warfare is accomplished, that her iniquity is pardon: for she hath received of the Lord's hand DOUBLE for all her sins." (Isaiah 40:1-2)

9

DO YOU HAVE GOOD CREDIT WITH GOD?

"A good name is rather to be chosen than riches."   *Proverbs 22:1*

CHAPTER NINE

Do You Have Good Credit With God?

For three years, while I was in the nest, I used to tell everybody that I was just a key "to be". I'm sure many thought that I was just making them laugh because of my comical nature. When I would say that, I truly felt something go through me. I never liked my name, "Keebee". When people would ask my name, after telling them I always got this negative response like, "What's A Keebee"? As God began do deal with me about my character and what he would do in me, he once told me that he was going to change my name. I know that this change had to do with my credibility and character and not my actual name. However, God did use my actual name to get my attention. He called me *Key-Be*. As time went on, the Lord asked me, Who doth men say that I am. I had no response, but when he asked me, "Who Do You Say That I Am?" I knew that God was going somewhere with this question.

The whole time that I was in the nest, some compared me with my spiritual sister Prophetess Bynum. At that time, it was so hard for me because I was struggling for my own identity and place in God. I was afraid of being made in the shadow of another. Finally, I realized that God had placed us under the same blood family. Our DNA was not our own making. We looked like our spiritual parents. We both were so different yet you could see the fruit of our spiritual parents flowing through us. We talked like them. We exposed demons like them. We prayed and travailed like them. This was a very strange experience in which I did not always understand. Many times I felt that the saints had not discerned the gift that was among them. I'm free now to say, "She is my sister."

We are all ultimately from the same anointing in God. However you can never fabricate and reproduce the same exact set of fingerprints. We are all uniquely made according to our own personal experiences and journeys. When my mentor, Vedar Nichols came to speak at my church convention in Philadelphia, many of the saints were amazed by what they saw. It was said to me that it was like listening to me. There should be some resemblances of you and your mentor. When mantles are passed from one person to the other it affects your spirit man for the most part. Not one time did my situations change and become identical to hers. I was still, me. I have always been a very dramatic and comical person. However, the ability to deal with the issues was more twin like than anything. However, impartations are real. This is important to remember when you are connected to individuals who are not godly as well. (Even if they are ministers, some are ungodly.)

When others would have certain expectations of me because of whom they thought I should be like, I allowed the enemy to put me in a certain state of bondage. I was afraid to flow in ministry because other people expected me to act like my sister. It was a very uncomfortable place to be in because I had my own deaths and hells that I had walked in. Wherever I would go people would call me by her name. I did not feel like an individual. This really made me feel intimidated about my future. I felt as if I was beaten with her name. In time I began to ask the Lord to reveal me. When God asked me, "Who Do You Say That I Am?" I understood that in order to know who I was, I needed to know who He was. I needed a revelation of His name and His person. When I understood who the "Christ" was, "The Anointed One", that's when God promised me the keys of the kingdom of heaven (which are binding and loosing), as he did with Peter in Matthew 16:19. There were other keys that he promised such as keys of wisdom, keys of faith, keys of love, etc. God used my name to get me to understand the process of how He was transforming me.

Back in 1994, while in the nest, he told me that he was making me a key and that I would unlock others. He was speaking of the deliverance ministry that he was forming inside of my spiritual womb. It's not a coincidence that when you deal with a persons name you're dealing with their character and credibility. When you go to a bank to get a loan, the bank officer always ask for your name. Your name is connected to your number that gives them access to your credit history. If credit is bad, then so is your name. As the Lord began to shape my life, he showed me that each notch that he cut out of me was shaping me for the future. He was making me a *key* vessel in the deliverance ministry. If your name is bad, then your signature can't get you a thing. If the credit bureau says that your name is bad, what it is saying about you is that, "You Lack Integrity". Your signature is what bound you to the contract. When you break the contract, you break your word. Not only is your word your bond, so is your name. God is looking to use those with integrity and honesty. You have to be a man or woman of your word. If God can't trust you with your own word, how can He entrust you with His. What does heaven's credit bureau have to say about your credit history? Does it call you a liar? Have you paid the cost or have you stolen another's cloak? You can't fake the anointing. If you haven't paid through death to your self then, you are premature and dangerous. While Jesus paid the price for your life, it's going to cost you something for the call. You need to take God's word and let it affect your word, that your word will become true. That's a good way to break the spirit of a liar off of your life, Walk in the word of God. Only God's word is true. Man's word is a lie.

When you stand against the enemy, the only name that he will bow to is the name of Jesus. When God began to change my name, I could feel a powerful transformation in my words and my mind. I began to take on the characteristics of Christ. It was no longer I that lived, but the Christ that lived in me. At this point, I knew that the Master was making me a copy of Himself. He is the Master Key, but I am a copy. I am still being shaped. When I call

My Jesus My Master, I can feel the foundation of hell shake. When I walk in the character and integrity of Jesus, I feel like one of those powerful keys that Jesus used to open death, hell and the grave and unlock life. God has called us all to be keys. I pray that you will have many keys on your key chain before it's over. Keys unlock and lock up. Jesus is my Master. I am his copy. God's keys are found in God's word. *Be A Key, Walk In Liberty And Set The Captives Free!*

FROM: JESUS, "YOUR GREAT EAGLE"

Just see me! Just see me!
No matter what you see, just stay free.
No matter what you see, you've got to see me.
Just see me! "I AM" Key.

See me and be free, just see me and Be a Key!
You're a copy of me, for "I AM" the key.
You be free, and just Be a Key!

So see me, I am with thee.
See me that I am in thee.
I've given you authority I've made you a key.
Be free! Cause you are a key.

Key to my joy, Key to my love,
Be a key, like me above.
Key to new life and liberty,
Be a Key and set my people free,

Just be key, Key-Be!
Just be key and set them free.
Their liberty depends on thee.
Stay "BE" and you will see.

I've formed you and shaped you to what I want you to be.
You are a key and that I see.

It matters to me, what I've called you to be.
Be a key and set my people free.
Just see me-just see me.
I see thee-you're a Key!
You're going to open doors and lock them too.
So many things that I will have you do.
You're going to make some see that they should be key.
You're going to cause them to want to be a copy of me.

10

PIERCING THE DARKNESS

"For God, who commanded the light to shine out of darkness, hath shined in our hearts, to give the light of the knowledge of the glory of God in the face of Jesus Christ."

2 Corinthians 4:6

CHAPTER TEN

Piercing The Darkness

In the beginning God created the heavens and the earth. And the earth was without form, and void; and *darkness* was upon the *face of the deep*. And the Spirit of God moved upon the face of the waters. And God said, "*let there be light*", and there was light. And God saw the Light, that it was good: and God divided the light from darkness. And God called the light day, and the darkness he called night. And the evening and the morning were the first day.

Whenever God speaks to me through his word, I try not to get stuck on that experience. I found out that God is even greater than my last experience with him. After being in the nest for about two years, God began to speak to me about the darkness that I was in. This was another level of darkness. I would write every word down that he spoke in my ear. Although, I did not fully understand what he was saying, I understood enough to know that I was in a place that *I referred to as hell*. It was a very dark place. Every once in a while I would gain enough insight just to move on to the next level. Each level bought with it a trial that left me in a dark place. At some point, God will send a small flash of light. This light was the fire of God. The Holy Spirit became my fire by night. I would go in and out of trials as one going in and out of darkness. The light would bring with it "a purity". I was forever burning. I mean it was a tangible anointing. This anointing was burning *through* me. It was a cleansing power. After the fire would lift, it always left me feeling as though I was being cleaned and sanctified. I got to the point that I felt as though I was being delivered from something constantly. Every time someone would tell me that it was my time, I would go through some form of deliverance. My *time* became a question in my mind. I wanted to know what did that really mean.

Later God began to reveal to me this level of darkness called, "Piercing the darkness". I had a vision of blackness that was so black that nothing could be seen. This blackness was covering me. When you are covered in darkness, you are placed out of sight. You are hidden, concealed and obscure. Suddenly, there appeared a small pinhole of light. It seemed to me to pierce that darkness. It allowed a small portion of light to penetrate and pass into or *through* it. I was able to discover some of the inner contents of this dark body and discern it deeply. It was as if darkness was covering the face of my spirit. I knew it wasn't in my spirit, but it certainly hovered over my spirit. Suddenly again, I saw more. There appeared to be many pinholes of light that formed a line as that of a perforation in black paper. It seemed to me that it could be torn apart. God told me that my breakthrough was coming and I would tear through the darkness.

He began to speak to me about the abilities of light. He said that light was nothing more than fire that was manifested in light. Fire burns, purifies, lights, destroys, and signals. It has the ability to burn through the darkness, purify your mind and destroy the darkness. It even signals those standing by. I found myself in this body of darkness that I referred to as hell. This body seemed to have a language. It spoke, but it only spoke lies. Spiritually speaking it had an odor, the stench of dead and rotting flesh. It had movement, as if it were enlarging herself.

> *"Therefore hell hath enlarged herself, and opened her mouth without measure: and their glory, and their multitude, and their pomp, and he that rejoiceth, shall descend into it."* (Isaiah 5:14)

There was war with the Angels of God and demonic forces all around me. It was militant and had order. Certain demons had more rank than others. Darkness had a mind of its own. Though hell was called dark, it could not comprehend light when it penetrated. Darkness was disabled when light was present. Light confused it.

"For this ye know, that no whoremonger, nor unclean person, nor covetous man, who is an idolater, hath any inheritance in the kingdom of Christ and of God. For ye were sometimes darkness, but now are ye light in the Lord: walk as children of light: (for the fruit of the spirit is in all goodness and righteousness and truth;) proving what is acceptable unto the Lord. And have no fellowship with the unfruitful works of darkness, but rather reprove them. For it is a shame even to speak of those things which are done of them in secret." (Ephesians 5:5,8-12)

There is a miracle working power that is released when light comes in contact with darkness. Light expels, dismisses, forces out, drives out, suspends, and nullifies darkness. The bible says that God is a consuming fire (Hebrews 12:29). He manifested His light through His son Jesus. He burns through the anointing, which is the personality of the Holy Ghost. The anointing is what destroys the yoke.

"For every one that doeth evil hateth the light, neither cometh to the light, lest his deeds should be reproved (exposed). But he that doeth truth cometh to the light, that his deeds may be made manifest, that they are wrought in God." (John 3:20-21)

I personally believe that sinners are in darkness, but they cannot enter *into it to see*. What I mean is they can't effectively expose it. They need the signal of fire, the light of God that shows them the lie and the truth. When no light is present, sight is impossible. Also, when no light is *pre-sent* (Light or Glory beforehand) sight is impossible. We are that light that has been pre-sent into the world. We *represent* Jesus. We represent the light that has already come and shall return. We signal them in the darkness when we let our light so shine before men, that they see our good works and want to glorify our God which is in heaven. As a child of God, we are walking through the darkness but we are not in darkness. When I was in this spiritual *place* called hell, God told me that I would not always walk in darkness, but I would walk *through* it. The word through is used as a function word to indicate movement into one side or point and out at another. It's from the beginning of something to the end of it. It is also the completion, conclusion or accomplishment of something. Finally, it indicates, into the open and then out - *BREAKTHROUGH.*

If you get into the opening of trouble, you can certainly find your way out of it. It's the way of escape that Jesus has made.

The weapons of our warfare are not carnal but they are mighty through God to the pulling down of strongholds. Within the word through, is the word rough. When something is rough, it is difficult to travel through or penetrate. It comes with violence or force. It presents you with a challenge. The bible says that the kingdom of God suffers violence, but the violent take it by force. When we take the kingdom, we pierce the darkness; we penetrate it by discerning it with the word of God. We perforate it and tear through its contents. The Light of God brings transparency into our lives. When I look back at my place of hell, I can see the darkness that hovered over the face of my spirit-the deepest part of me. The Spirit of God moved upon the face of the waters that were deep within my spirit. The face of a person (in this case my spirit man which is the real me) is the outer seen portion of the head. The head is the heaviest part of the body. The head houses the vision, the eyesight, the hearing, the nostrils and speaking capacities. The eyes of your spirit, sees with the eyes of God. The ears of your spirit, Hears the word of the Lord. The nostrils of your spirit, breathes with the breathe of life. The covering for the head of your spirit is Jesus Christ. In the head of your spirit are the thought and the mind of God. The thoughts of God are words in His mind. Jesus is the Word made manifest in you.

"Be careful for nothing; but in every thing by prayer and supplication with thanksgiving let your requests be made known unto God. And the peace of God, which passeth all understanding, shall keep your hearts and minds through Christ Jesus. Finally, brethren, whatsoever things are true, whatsoever things are honest, whatsoever things are just, whatsoever things are pure, whatsoever things are lovely, whatsoever things are of good report; if there be any praise, think on these things." (Philippians 4:6-8)

The Holy Spirit wanted to abide fully in me but the oppression was present. I had a will to live in the spirit realm, but all hell was present even as the Spirit of God moved. There was a battle in me, and a war going on. I was without form and I was void. I was empty. But as I began to listen with the ears of my spirit I could hear God say, "LET - THERE - BE - LIGHT": and there was light. This was God piercing the darkness with his word. The darkness was apparent in the way I thought. My mind needed renewal. God saw the light, and that it was good. And God divided the Light from the Darkness within me. He cleared my conscience. He divided my soul and my spirit and showed me what was of God and what was not. He put things in order. He called the light day, and the darkness he called night. And the evening and the morning were the first day of my life. For me this was the breaking of day. When I refer to the face of the deep, I am referring to the face of my spirit. I had a darkened conscience. Darkness was upon the face of my spirit, not in it, but upon it. It kept me blind. The eyes of my understanding were dim. When you are blind, you cannot see. You have no clear vision. The bible says that without a vision, the people perish. True worshippers don't perish. They see because they hear. They hear because they seek. They seek because they are sought after-by their God. They are sought after, because God is looking for such " *The True Worshippers*".

As each trial bought with it, a piercing light, I can see how God Almighty tore right through those perforations and destroyed the works of darkness that was within my soul. He perforated the darkness according to His divine word and separated it. When the Light of God broke through the darkness, I broke through. I had a *breakthrough!* The anointing of God destroyed the yoke (the shells) that bound my mind. My mind was transformed with renewal of God's word of light. It was renewed and still being renewed back to the original state that God intended it to be prior the fall of man. This is now allowing me to see what the good, and acceptable, and perfect, will of God is for my life.

All Christians need to understand that they are triune beings. We are really spirits that live in a body, and we possess a soul. Our spirits are made in the image of God. This is where the Holy Spirit abides when He comes in. Our spirit man is the perfect man when God dwells there. It is eternal, and will live somewhere forever, depending on what master you choose (God or Satan). Our bodies are nothing more than a housing unit or a shell. It is flesh and will rot away. Flesh is flesh, and spirit is spiritual. Flesh is not eternal. Our soul man is made of our will, reasoning, thinking, and decision-making processes. It is the devil's battleground of spiritual warfare. The enemy attacks the mind to make his strike. This is why it is important that the mind of man be transformed and renewed. We are led many times by our minds, but we should be led by the Spirit of God-that lives within us. I believe that my spirit is king, my soul is servant and my body is slave. Kings are known to be masters. If Jesus Christ lives in you, you should be ruling. You are of a royal family. Royalty is for you. The bible calls us believers a Holy Nation and Royal Priesthood. If you want to reign in the

Kingdom of God, you must understand who you are in Christ Jesus. *Do you know who you are? Let There Be Light!*

Thorns In My Nest

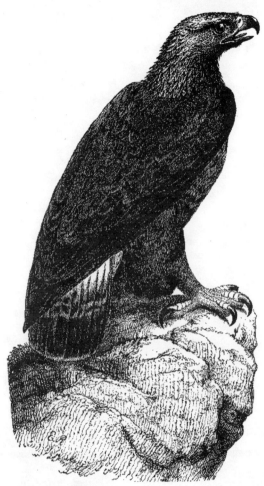

11

GOD'S ABOUT TO INDUCE YOUR LABOR

"Enlarge the place of thy tent, and let them stretch forth the curtains of thine habitations: spare not, lengthen thy cords, and strengthen thy stakes; For thou shalt break forth on the right hand and on the left; and thy seed shall inherit the Gentiles, and make the desolate cities to be inhabited."

Isaiah 54:2-3

CHAPTER ELEVEN

God's About To Induce Your Labor

After the kiss of Judas and partaking of the forbidden fruit, the enemy had me thinking that I had lost my spiritual baby. I thought it was over. I thought God would never use me, *a failure*. Mistaken by my warring thoughts, I found out that I had broken fellowship with God, but not relationship. I gave up on man (which is what I needed to do), but I did not give up on God. The cord was broken, but the blood was in place. It was covenant and it was by blood. God knew, God saw, God restored and God forgave. The Housekeeper came Himself to clean my house. He sent no one, Jesus showed up *face to face. For this I humbly thank you, Lord.*

The kiss of Judas will induce your spiritual labor. The kiss will bring to your attention loose baggage that you are carrying. These loaded bags are things that are prohibited in destiny and ministry. The kiss had a purpose and God used it for His cause. Even though I fell along the way, with much remorse, God was still faithful to his word. His only requirement was that I repent...and with a spirit of brokenness I fell on my face before God. Drawn in by the Spirit of God, the Housekeeper rescued my wounded soul from a literal hell.

By God's divine grace and mercy, the call of God for my life was still His priority and His mandate. With the help that I received from the divine kiss, I was forced into an induction state of prayer to bring forth the ministry from within my spiritual womb. Induction brings on pain-*suddenly*. Before I knew it, I was in the transition stage of labor in position to push in a spiritual sense (laying before God in travailing prayer). When this stage of prayer was on, It did not appear to be nice and beautiful, like a woman in natural labor. All hell breaks loose in the birthing room and it is somebody else's fault that she's in the predicament that she's in, "*pregnant*"...and she makes that powerful declaration to never do it again. And of course when she's close to delivery, she doesn't feel too attractive.

Although my oversized spiritual belly made me wobble with instability and double mindedness, I knew that after spiritual deliverance this miserable walk would balance itself.

I had taken in the vitamins of his word. I had drink much water in the spirit through worship. I had even exercised in the step aerobic of faith. The baby's weight was just right (I was quite heavy), not too big and not too small. The head of what I knew as ministry was positioned for the crown to come forth. Many things of the past had surfaced. The obstetrician of my spirit had figured the exact delivery date. His time, not mine and certainly not mans. He visited me and broke my waters when he came in as the housekeeper.

It was in his time and right on time. Now it was time to push as some say it, *"Pray-Until-Something-Happens"*. I felt a great urge to do so.

Though the pain was great, it was that final thrust of the kiss of Judas that helped me to stoop into the position of prayer and push out that last gust of waters and bring forth *my baby*, "***The ministry of forgiveness, the power to love, the joy of the morning, and the anointing to deliver***". The push bought about a pain of relief. (It is a relief when you let go of things that burden you down). You know the sound in the delivery room, "*It's a boy!*!! Well, here it is, "*It's a ministry-* one of reconciliation, restoration and healing!!! This baby is my ministry. The pain of that labor was great, but I've literally forgotten what each contraction felt like as I touch the precious parts of this special little bundle and kiss his fat cheeks. It seems to me that this chunky little fellow received well from the spiritual placenta that was in place to give him food. God kept, God fed, and God saved my ministry.

As a natural mother of four precious children, I know the feeling and excitement of seeing that baby when it breaks forth into day. My God, what a bundle of joy! No matter what your baby looks like, all you see is beauty. No matter what anyone else sees, you are focused. There is a pure love for, "Your baby" and a passion to embrace it God's way. Immediately you forget the pain of delivery and enjoy the fruit of your womb.

It is this seed, even as you read it, that will and has bruised the head of my enemy. Now I can say, "Satan, go directly to hell.

Do not past go, do not collect $200". If the enemy is going to play the game of monopoly over your life, he'd better be ready to loose. *You are a winner!* While he's gambling with your life, God has already *invested* too much into your land to allow the enemy to land on you and win. He may land on you at times, but he will not have the victory over your life. You are God's investment, not mans. God uses man as a vessel to mentor and train, but it is the work of the Lord working in you and through you. Too much has been built in and on you. The devil must pay the price for treading on your grounds. It will cost him big! God has broken him to pieces. He's run out of cash. *The game is over and the buck stops **here**!!!*

Isn't it like an eagle to allow her young to leave the nest and stand in waiting, to swoop down and catch that baby while she's about to kill herself in a fall. Before she dies, there she finds herself rested on the wing of her Great Eagle, "Jesus". That's when *Mercy found me, Mercy caught me, Mercy healed me, and Mercy delivered me! I now know mercy and I now know love.* As one pastor put it, "Mercy understood is holiness desired". My ultimate desire is Jesus. There's not enough that you could do to make Him stop loving you. Be careful saints of God! Don't throw out the trash too fast. Know what to throw out and know what to recycle. God has a special way of recycling the junk that you reject. That dirty old soda container could someday be a Range Rover. True love will correct you, rebuke you, reprove you and keep on loving you.

He is a God of wrath, and of Mercy. You cannot separate His love from His Mercy. You cannot separate His Mercy from

His Grace. This is why it is so important that Jesus is the center focus of your life. When He arrived on the scene in the form of man, so did Grace. If you are born again, you are covered in the blood of Jesus. Particularly when there is true repentance and brokenness. When the angels see the blood, they cry M-E-R-C-Y!!! Goodness and Mercy follows you all the days of your life. His word is true. Whatever he has spoken, it shall not return unto him void. He will do what He said He's going to do in your life.

12

RESERVATION IN THE "INN"

"For I say unto you, that except your righteousness shall exceed the righteousness of the scribes and Pharisees, ye shall in no case enter into the kingdom of heaven."

Matthew 5:20

Chapter Twelve

Reservation In The "Inn"

I AM YOUR HOUSEKEEPER

Your righteousness is as filthy rags. Just as the housekeeper comes to collect your dirty towels, that's what I've come to do. I expect you to come before me asking and receiving anew. Give me your rags of filth - rags of pride, rags of guilt, rags of unforgiveness, rags of stubbornness (which is as witchcraft), rags of hatred, prejudice and bitterness. I've even come for your rags of sin, evil works and evil thoughts. I'll take your rags of biasness and unjust attitudes and I'll give you mine anew. Daily ye shall receive of me but, only as you ask. I'll freshen your laundry with scents of morning dew filled with love, scents of fresh rain pouring out in health and wealth. Take on me. I am not a one-time medicine. You need me always for life and healing. I'll heal your thoughts with the freshness of My Word. I'll wash your dirt with the brightness of my blood. Let me bleach out the stains from past hurts and disappointments. Let me use my softener as I ply you in my hand. I'll keep your heart soft with the scents of the freshness of my spirit. Come unto me *"You"* who labor and are heavy burdened and I will give you rest.

I AM YOUR HOUSEKEEPER

You are the house, the building, the residence, the abode and the dwelling place. I am the housekeeper, the custodian, and the keeper of your soul. I have custody of you. I am your guardian and you're in my care. Do you know that your body is the temple of the Holy Spirit, who is in you, whom you have received from God? You are not your own; you were bought at a price. Therefore honor God with your body.

I AM YOUR HOUSEKEEPER

There are things in the *"INN"* my *"QUALITY INN"* (that's you), that I, your housekeeper will not touch because they are your personal belongings. Those things you must straighten out even as I the Lord will show you. I will show you and you shall do them in my strength. All things will be done through me. *Get your house in order.* There are things in the "Quality Inn" that I have already paid for. It's in the price. Cleansers for cleaning, my word will wash you as white as snow. Conditioners to keep your heart soft, I've called you to a life of prayer and worship. There's even a phone to make the call. Call me! I will hear you. I've provided for you light and lamps within the inn to show you the way of the right path. My light shines in dark places. To receive the light, you must turn on the power. The power is there for your authority and force in the spirit. The Kingdom of God suffereth violence and the violent take it by force. There's a table prepared for you in the presence of your enemies. Even as the natural inn provides a continental breakfast, so do I. Only in the morning my mercies are renewed. Come before me early. Come, eat my body and drink my blood. I am the bread of life. Seek me early while I may be found. There is fire for light and heat. Even as the inn reserves a refrigerator for the storage of food, I have prepared your heart for that purpose. Hide my word in your heart that you will not sin against me. Storing my word in your heart will keep you safe from poisoning and spiritual bacterial. For your rest, I have provided a bed for your comfort. Rest in me. Make me your nest for rest. Take in the breath of life from the fresh air that I blow when the temperatures are raised. There are even clean windows to keep the vision clear. Clarity means everything in my Kingdom. See through the eyes of the Spirit.

And finally, I have provided for thee water to drink. While the water in this inn is not nice looking, it's not harmful. Just let the water run, It will clear up. Drink of my Spirit! My waters are pure but it is you that has the taint because of your human nature. As you drink of me I will clear up every tainted spot in your pipe. I will remove every hard water stain that was left from past hurts and rejections. I will remove all deposits and build ups that are not of me. Receive me, because I am your portion. Many things I find when I come to clean your house. To men these things are not pleasing to the eye, but to me it is an opportunity to set you free. I will carry away the trash, and wash every spot clean. Just trust me, *I AM YOUR HOUSEKEEPER*. The enemy comes to kill, steal and destroy. I AM come that you might have life and have it more abundantly.

There are days that I come to take your dirty laundry and you say, "No Not Today!" My child, please do not put out your *"DO NOT DISTURB"* sign. Other times you say to me, "I will do it." But my child, I stand at the door and knock. Here I am. If anyone hears my voice and opens the door, I will come in and eat with him and he with me. *(Rev 3:20)* You don't have the power to clean, for you need what I have. *I AM THE HOUSEKEEPER*. When you say, " I'll do it myself, "know that you must depend on me for I know all things and I... only I can make you clean. Any time you separate me from my blood, you loose power. I come with the blood. My Father and I are one. Receive me and you receive Him. Have me and you'll have Him. Don't take the power of the blood from me but let us (Father, Son and Holy Spirit), make you whole. My blood is a whitener that bleaches out the toughest stains of life.

I AM YOUR HOUSEKEEPER

YOU ARE MY QUALITY INN. I have made you *VALUABLE* with the price that I paid by giving my life for your sins. I made you a *PECULIAR* person. I have given you *GRADE* with the *SPIRIT OF EXCELLENCE*. You have *CALIBER* and *CHARACTER* because you're made in *MY*

IMAGE. You have *DISTINCTION* because you are known by my love. You have *RANK* because I am the one who have positioned you. You have *STATUS* because you're seated in heavenly places in Christ Jesus. And yes, I have *MARKED* you with the blood of my son Jesus Christ. You don't have to feel inferior, move in mediocrity, or become indifferent. You don't even have to live as a second rate, having no being, substance or essence. You are *QUALITY,* and therefore are *QUALIFIED,* equipped and empowered to be *MY QUALITY INN.*

JESUS

These are the words that the Lord spoke to me while staying in a hotel in Coldwater, Michigan. Having been kissed by my divine friend Judas, I found myself in a cold place, feeling as though death had taken me over twice. Only moving on a small still voice that lingered in my spirit while I slept. I could hear the silence say, **"It's not over until God says it's over."** I could imagine when Jesus died, there had to be at least a tiny bit of his blood left somewhere on him or in him. He couldn't do nothing but resurrect because, the power of his own blood was even in the grave. Because God had marked me with his blood, the ground that the enemy had buried me in, was crying out. When the devil harms you, "*The blood cries out*". (Remember Cain and Abel)?

185

I slept a deep sleep until the Lord visited my gravesite. He came in such a gentle way. He walked ever so lightly in my spiritual house as He cleaned it. It was a *quiet* and powerful visitation. His knock at my heart was so light that I had to be completely still to hear the Father's voice. I sat for hours just listening to His voice. He never screamed, He was never rude, but He was firm and gentle. He was a *"gentle giant"*. His touch was so deep within my mind and spirit that I woke up daily, waiting for Him to come in. Although, I wanted my spiritual parents to come and get me, God Himself showed up at my doorstep. The Lord wanted to deliver me with His mighty hand. No one was to get the glory. The experience reminded me of a tree that I once saw lying on its side. Though it had fallen, the roots were somehow still attached to the soil. Every leaf budded in the spring though it appeared to be dead. The waters were still flowing giving it moisture. It received light even while stretched out in the forest. Not one leaf withered.

Though I had myself fallen, for some reason, I could not die. Nothing could stop me. I was destined to *Be A Key*. This is another time that I heard the voice of the Lord speak to me and said, "*Key-Be*". In other words, "*Be A Key*". When I heard the Lord call me by name, He knocked at the door of my heart and introduced Himself as "*The Housekeeper.*" When I recognized who He was, immediately I gave Him my undivided attention. Every day for six weeks He visited me. Later, I realized that the Lord spoke to this great fish that He had prepared (as He did with Jonah), and it vomited me up.

"And the Lord spake unto the fish, and it vomited out Jonah upon the dry land."

(Jonah 2:10)

As my husband and daughter would leave the hotel for work and school, the Holy Spirit came to deliver a Word. He told me to go and clean a small church in Coldwater, Michigan. I gave myself to that ministry and cleaned it as if I was on another mission. The people probably wondered where did this black woman come from (It was a church with only Caucasians). The Lord had earlier spoken to me that I was to clean that church. I had no idea that the pastor would announce that they needed a housekeeper on that very day. God met me each time as I gave myself to this small body of believers who didn't know a thing about me. God allowed the Pastors of that beautiful ministry to entrust me with a "Key" to enter and clean after each service. That key to me represented the keys of deliverance and authority that God was about to entrust me with. He gave me keys of deliverance to assist in cleaning the spots on the garments of His church. I pushed dirt devils until they ate their own dust. I remember telling the enemy to *"Bite The Dust"* as I pushed that vacuum cleaner. I scrubbed bathrooms until I heard God say, *"Flush*

Your Stuff. I cleaned that church the way the Lord was cleaning me. I submitted as if this was my home base yet, enjoying the Love of God that poured out of the people of God.

Coincidently, *"so I thought"*, one of the housekeepers that cleaned my room on a daily basis, happened to be a member of that church. After about three weeks of meeting in my room under the power of the Holy Ghost, she realized that I was the cleaning lady at her church. As God met me each morning, He not only set me free but He would use me to minister to the housekeepers that would come to my room. They started coming to my room just to get in His presence daily.

I can hear the Lord saying to you, "I want to come In the Inn. I want to lodge, dwell, live, occupy, inhabit, abide and settle in you. If you will give me a place to rest, I will lay in you. But first allow me to clean your house. When you give me your rags, I'll give you mine. I will dress you. My rag is the Robe of Righteousness. I will take you from rags to riches. My riches will prosper your spirit, soul and body. Allow me to lay it on you, that is—my coat, "The Robe of Righteousness". In me you will live, move and have your being.

I AM YOUR HOUSEKEEPER

"But I will sacrifice unto thee with the voice of thanksgiving; I will pay that that I have vowed. Salvation is of the Lord." (Jonah 2:9)

13

LET THE WATERS RUN

"Out of the same mouth proceedeth blessing and cursing. My brethren these things ought not so to be. Doth a fountain send forth at the same place sweet water and bitter?"

James 3:10-11

CHAPTER THIRTEEN

Let The Waters Run

*"I will make you a fountain of life, says the Lord your God.
As many touch you and come in contact with what's in you,
I will cause them to be changed. They shall be transformed.
Lead them to this place. Bring them into my presence.
Pull them from the fire. As they look for another,
I shall show up in their paths. I shall shine forth out of the dark.
I shall reveal to them a new way, a new place, and a new life. Pray for
them. Pray much for them. As you stay consistently in my presence, I
will fill you with my Spirit and life more abundantly whereas it will be too
much for you. Out of your belly shall it-flow. Your flow shall be living
and powerful, able to remove death, causing life to spring forth. It will be
a great river.
For in the center of my will is a perpetual fountain of Glory."
Jesus said, "If any man thirst, let him come unto me, and drink.
He that believeth on me, as the scripture hath said, out of his belly shall
flow rivers of living water. John 7:37-38*

In 1991, the Lord visited me in a dream. In the dream I was wrapped in white fine linen. On top of this material, I had on a very soft white linen skirt in which the hands and wrist of Jesus appeared at my knees. I could see the wounds where Jesus was nailed to the cross. It appeared that He was touching my knees. Underneath this skirt I was clothed from my neck down to my ankles with white linen material that was gathered together all over my body. In my hand was the Sword of the Spirit. Jesus said to me, "*You're next.*" After waking from my sleep, "I kept asking God what did that mean?" He revealed to me that the clothes represented the word of God. Eventually, he led me to Ezekiel 47. This chapter speaks of the vision of the *Holy Waters!* My God, that was so powerful to me. God told me the waters were rising and it was at my knees. He showed me that the water represented His Spirit. He also said that this was a season of prayer for me.

During this time the Lord birth in me a spirit of prayer. He taught me how to intercede for others. I had never heard of anyone being birth through. But, the Holy Ghost was praying through me with words that could not be uttered. For the sake of discipline God called me to pray at 3:00am every morning. I did not make this time a "*Doctrine of Religion*" because I wanted to stay open to the moving of the Holy Spirit. Religion can become a spirit that tries to figure out how God is going to move next. God prefers relationship rather than religion. Therefore, when it lifted off of me to stop praying at 3:00am, I started praying whenever I was led to.

I learned to pray for my leaders, my church and many others as the Spirit of God led me. This also began to work out something in my own character. It kept me sensitive and softened within my heart. There were some days that I found myself praying for hours as the Spirit of the Lord would visit my house and literally command a Holy Hush in quiet time. God's presence was so strong that I would lay slain in the spirit for moments and hours at a time. I learned to drink in the spirit during these moments of quietness. I learned to hear and listen. Solitude was mine. Sometimes, I find that when I am too loud, I am not listening, (even in my thoughts). God desires to speak when we are sometimes talking, even in prayer. Learn to embrace the power of silence. Much of my deliverance has been a quiet and deep experience in the glory of God instead of a loud bang. However, I've experienced both. When the glory of God comes, it is His turn to talk, not ours.

There are times when I feel the arms and hands of God wrap Himself around me, as if I am an only child for the moment. His love for us is so great and deep. *Embrace Him in His Holy chambers.* Not every one that confesses to know the Lord Jesus Christ really know Him. To know him is to be intimate with Him. To know Him is to get in His face until His glory overshadows you. To know Him is to become so intimate with Him that you become impregnated with purpose and destiny. When you get in His face you will take on His characteristics. His love will be your love. His vision will become your vision. You will no longer see yourself or others in the flesh. You will see them as Jesus sees them, through

His precious blood. Come apart and separate yourself for a time alone with him. Experience the power of *Divine Worship*. Drink in His presence. His living waters will give you life. *Death must only live long enough to move out of your way!* You shall live and not die to declare the works of the Lord.

I command the enemy of death to *move*. Anything dead can't move. Therefore, I believe God's power is so great that it will give death enough life just to get out of your way. Apparently, the devil doesn't know who you are. Let me correct that, He does know who you are and that is the problem. When God pours himself into you the devil and all of his angels will know it. Get up! *You Are Somebody!!! The devil knows your name and he is mad about it.*

Lord, I want a drink from your fountain of life. Fill me until the waters are too deep to swim in. Let me become so saturated in your Spirit that I am soaked in pools of Mercy, Love, forgiveness and Power. I am so thirsty for your liquid love, liquid light, liquid strength and mercy. I need your fluids of life to live. As blood to the body is life and it is liquid, so... the blood of Jesus to my life is the same, LET THE SPIRIT FLOW.

Lord, I don't seek you because I'm called. I seek you because I need the ministry of your Glory. I need the ministry of your divine presence. I have no ministry until your presence minister to me. I cannot minister until you give me the ministry of yourself. I learn to give you me, as you give me you. You don't love me because I love you. I love you because you first loved me. The anointing that you use in me to set others free, use it to keep me free. Have mercy on me and sustain me Lord. It is not I that live but you that live in me.

Without you O Lord, I am truly nothing. My bones were as dust and my heart was bitter and void. Only you can and have healed my broken heart. You are a great deliverer and in you I will put my trust. In times of deep hurt and pain you visited me. Your presence to me was like that of a life support. You breathed and I had life. You pumped and the blood of Jesus flowed. Even in my wrongdoing mercy found me. Grace softly melted my pride and dealt with the inner most part of my being.

I was like a child without a breast for suck and you lifted me up and fed me from your own body. I was abandoned and left for dead, and you washed me white as snow. I had no identity until you gave me yours. Now I carry your name Jesus. When my choices were twisted and misleading, you took the time to make the crooked places straight. When my childhood damaged my mind, you ordered my steps to walk in your word. When men misused and abused my womanhood, you touched the wounds that no one has ever touched. You fathered me and gave me a reason to be. You set standards and commanded me to stand. Not only did I stand, you caused me to understand. You placed the word of God under my stand.

You revealed to me the truth about true womanhood and exposed what a man really is. You taught me in your way and broke the curses of my past. You slammed the enemy of deception and allowed truth to reign. How can I not praise you? How can I even question the work of your mighty hand? How can I question the design of my nest? My nest is now my crown. You have caused the bad to work for my good. My complaints have ceased and my praises for you are elevated. These praises are not of many words, because there aren't enough words to tell you how I feel. So My Lord and My God, without much to say, I sit in AWE of you.

Key-Be

When I was a Child...

You heard me when I didn't know that I was praying.
You touched me when I didn't know that I was being touched.
I wanted **You** when I didn't know it was **You** that I wanted.
You had taught me when I thought I had no understanding.

I desired **You** when I didn't know what I desired.
Your presence was with me when no one wanted to be in **Your** face.
I cried for You when I didn't know what I was crying for.
I heard Your voice when the rain would hit my house.

When it stormed, I heard **You** say, "Get ready!"
I worshipped **You** although I said, not a word.
You were in my thoughts when my words could not form **Your** name.
When I had no church home, **You** made me a tabernacle.

When transportation was none, there were angels to carry me.
When no one wanted to go, I looked for a way to get there.
Days before Sunday, I had already had church.
When I couldn't express me, **You** expressed "**Yourself**" instead.

When I feared death, **You** showed me life eternal.
Resurrection Sunday would come, but it was more than Easter to me.
When Satan kneeled by my bed, **You** rescued me from my enemy.
When my fears were great, **You** became my faith.

I sought after **You**, but me, **You** were already seeking.
I hungered for **You**, but my stomach **You** had already fed.
I ate **You** when I thought I was eating bread.
I drank of **You** when I thought I was drinking water.

With fire **You** baptized me when I was only eight.
When I went down in the water, there was fire when I came up.
When I arose out of the water, I came up with tears of brokenness.
In the quiet times **You** spoke words of encouragement to me.

Your 23 Psalms were the first words of my lips...

*When I was a child
It was You, Lord.*

Thorns In My Nest

14

THE RECOVERY ROOM

"And they overcame him by the blood of the Lamb, and by the word of their testimony; and they loved not their lives unto the death."

Revelation 12:11

CHAPTER FOURTEEN

The Recovery Room

After five months of letting the Housekeeper "*Jesus*" clean my house, he told me to get under a covering. He said, "I am going to establish you". Still sore from the wounds that I'd suffered, I went to this small church of all nations black, white, red, brown, etc. It was shepherded by an Italian couple in the City of Brotherly Love, Philadelphia. I sat on the first seat of the second row. I covered my head with an old leather cap. I wore jeans and sneakers that made me appear to look like I was from the hood. I had taken medication that was given to me in the emergency room the night before. The medication caused deep drowsiness and I appeared to be demonically possessed. I could feel the eyes of those around me staring me down. I did not want any one to know who I was. If God were going to ever use me again, it would definitely be His own doing. I was afraid of getting close to people. I had made up my mind that I didn't want any friends, for every one looked like Judas to me. I never wanted to be kissed again.

In that service there stood a young lady singing "*I am not ashamed of the gospel of Jesus Christ*". Her name was Francine. I hadn't been in a church for a while. At that moment, that was a good song to begin with. I lifted up my hands as I felt the presence of the Lord in the room. I swayed as my hands went into the air because of the medication. I could feel people looking at me as if to say, "What is wrong with her?" But frankly, I really did not care. At the end of the service, I waited around for a little while because I just wanted someone to lay hands on me and pray. The lady that I asked to pray for me gently refused because of fear, but she led me to a woman, "*The Pastor's Wife*" (Pastor Anne Scorsone). She prayed for my illness. Of course, the devil again was telling me, you are about to die.

When I left the service, I ended up in the emergency room on the next day. By Tuesday morning, I was being led to the operating room. I was very fearful of surgery. I was afraid that I would never wake up again. I requested that I not see the doctor who would perform the surgery. I just wanted to wake up and it was over with. There stood a male nurse who coached me as I shook with chills out of fear. I couldn't imagine having my belly opened completely up and taking a part of me out, the old fashioned way. When the nurse rolled me into the operating room, he gently laughed and talked with me while fumbling with wires and different things around me. He comforted me with such passion and care. I did not realize it, but he was slowly and gently putting me to sleep. What seemed like seconds was hours. I opened my eyes crying in pain as the anesthesia had worn off. I just kept saying oh my stomach, oh my stomach. I could hear someone calling my name as I struggled out of this deep sleep that they had put me in. When reality set in, I had been healed by way of surgical removal of that infected organ.

After some time, I returned to that little church and this time with my husband. As we set there, my husband whispered in my ear and said, "*This is our new church home.*" People greeted me and asked, "Where have you been?" I told them about my surgery and that was that. I sat in that church Sunday after Sunday until one day the Lord said, **"*Get up and testify!*"** I set there struggling with the Lord. I told him that I'll testify but I won't tell anybody anything about the call of God on my life. I will not let them know. God agreed of course! I asked the pastor if I could give a small testimony. I don't know why this little Italian man (Pastor Carl Scorsone) gave this black woman (who was dressed like she was from the hood) the microphone, I don't know why. Once I began to speak, I tried to give the microphone back to the pastor. He would not take it from me. When I looked up, I was preaching, prophesying and breaking curses of darkness off of people. The anointing of God was in the house. I knew without doubt that it was God. Before I knew it, it was over and God had pierced the darkness and uplifted the pastors in a mighty way.

When I set down, I asked God, "Why did you do that?" I said, "I told you, I did not want anybody to know who I was." It was truly a pure Word from the Lord because I did not know these people. When I got home that day, the Lord told me that I did not have to worry about the pain of the past anymore. He told me that he had placed me under the power and put me to sleep and he had removed the diseased parts from the past (He reminded me of the physical surgery). He said, " I did not allow you to see my face as I healed you because I knew how much you could take. Then He said, "*IT IS FINISHED*"! *Old things have past away and behold all things have become new.*" You talk about a year of Jubilee. My year wasn't just a "Jubilee", My way of life became a Jubilee. My mind was set free. I began to walk in the newness of life. God is Faithful. Bethel was like a recovery room for me. I had already had spiritual surgery before I went there, but God allowed me to recover and gain strength in that ministry by using my wings of faith. This was my recovery room. When the enemy tried to destroy the beauty of the feathers of my wings, God allowed my wings to be repaired and tested them in flight to build my confidence. *In quietness and confidence shall also be your strength.*

There in that ministry, my husband and I built an altar to the Lord. We planned in our hearts to be a blessing. The Lord strengthened us to submit to those leaders, Pastors Carl and Anne Scorsone. We committed ourselves and took on the vision of the pastor. God blessed us there. There was some warfare for me, but what *the nest* had to offer gave me strength. Confidence was my strength.

When God, My Great Eagle ordained me in the "House of God", I counted it A privilege to have The Eagle Known As, "Mom" present to lay hands on me and speak into my life as I was ordained. God had recently healed the wound in our relationship and cut off the head of the enemy that tried to destroy God's plan for us. Restoration had finally come. I saw God take a baby eagle and throw her up. This was a slap in the face of my enemy called, "Deception".

In The Recovery Room, You Recover...

ALL!

"Satan, I take the time to tell you, it's still not over.   May the blood of Jesus break every future attempt to stop me".

Thorns In My Nest

15

FREEDOM UNDER FIRE

"God is a spirit: and they that worship Him must worship Him in spirit and in truth."

John 4:24

CHAPTER FIFTEEN

Freedom Under Fire

As I arrived in the flight of ministry, I found myself in the small town of Pottstown, Pennsylvania. Although, there was a move of God in my spiritual belly for this town, I ran into some major obstacles. Until I got in the face of God, I was unable to detect what spiritual forces I was battling with. This warfare was extremely demonic. The spirit of Leviathan and the spirit of Jezebel were using individuals that had covetous appetites for success, to attack myself as well as others. (Remember, Satan needs a human body to carry out his plan to get the ultimate effectiveness). My aim was not to succeed as the world viewed success. My aim was to see Jesus face to face and experience the power of His glory and lead others behind the veil of God. Seeking God was and still is my mission. The Bible says...

"*But Seek ye first the kingdom of God, and His righteousness; and all these things shall be added unto you.*"
(Matthew 6:33)

Success and prosperity is not an evil idea. It is a God idea. Men make it evil with their selfish, evil motives. Don't seek Him because you want what's in His hand. Seek Him because *"you've got to have Him"*. Prosperity is for God's people. However, we should never seek things. Things cannot keep you. Seek God He is a keeper! Personally, I am more concerned with the spiritual state of God's people. I don't like to see ignorant Christians. If you know Jesus for whom He really is, He will show you how to get wealth with integrity. He will give you witty inventions with creativity. (God desires that we prosper spirit, soul and body). Set your heart to experience God's glory. Make it your hearts desire.

As for myself, I want God and I have to have him. I am addicted to His face. I want to know every part of the face of God, including the strength of His jawbone against my enemies. The face of God is the part that turns when we are not pleasing in His sight. When I step into the face of God, I want to know that He is giving me a righteous wink with thumbs up saying, "Well done my good and faithful servant, well done". I want to have such a relationship with God that when He gives me a certain look I can read His mind and interpret His heart. His face directs me. He face corrects me. His face gives me a certain look that says stop, go or do it no more. I want to know Him face to face. This is what I refer to as "*In your face ministry*". If He never gives me another thing, He has done enough for me. I will still thank Him. I will still love him and I will continue to run after Him. Furthermore, I give Him the glory for what He has already done.

When you are dealing with the presence and the face of God, you are dealing with the *glory of God*. The glory of God automatically brings with it the *truth of God*. God's glory cannot lie. God's glory cannot deceive. God's glory cannot and will not mislead. It is the manifested presence of Himself. His glory is in and of Himself. Within Himself is truth magnified. It is quite impossible to experience God behind the veil, if you walk in total deception. Because of my experience in the face of God, I was able to allow God to properly expose the demonic forces that I met in Pottstown. This town is where God gave me orders to "Take His Glory Back to the City".

Upon my arrival in the City of Pottstown, I did not know what was lying ahead, but I was prepared for the fight and always one step ahead of the enemy's game. You have to know your stuff to stay ahead of Satan. The spiritual community in this city had battled many issues before I arrived. I certainly was not their problem. They had their own issues that lingered from years of warring within as they battled with deep traditions that nullify the Word of God. Spirits of religion, adultery within church leadership, fallen and wicked leaders, and an extremely fierce spirit of deception had infiltrated that town. Many Christians there had given up on what we call church. In fact, at one point it was very difficult to minister under such a cloud of heaviness and darkness. Territorial demons such as, the spirit of Leviathan, a snake spirit, was out to eat them alive and swallow them whole. Rejection, intimidation, competitive jealousy, and other spirits dwelled there as well. These spirits were manifested under this ugly demon called, "Leviathan" known as the "*king of pride*". However, God has now begun to open the airways and destroy those strongholds to allow those who are walking in truth to minister with a greater impact.

The spirit of Leviathan is found Job chapter 41. It is a scaly spirit. The scales represent pride. It is also a slick, smooth operating spirit. The overlapped scales are what make it smooth. This spirit flows with much pride. As it uses individuals, it takes them through a molten process, in which they shed skins by mimicking change or transformation. Because Leviathan's prey, are usually ignorant of scripture, they are easily deceived into thinking change has occurred. During this shedding period, the individual appears to be repenting by apologizing to look humble. It will even admit some wrongdoing, but always leave out a portion of the truth because of its hidden motive. However, when Leviathan comes back he has a stronger rattle. Each shed makes the rattle louder because it leaves additional scales on the end of a snakes tail.

The split tongue of this spirit bites in the most hideous ways with its deadly words of lethal poison. It shoots out words of venom to go for the kill. (*It is done in the name of God*). Beware of

Leviathan the snake. It wants you dead. It wants to slowly wrap its body around you until you are squeezed to death by stopping your breath and cutting off your blood flow. It also poisons the blood with venom. Remember, blood is life. This spirit comes after the blood, but remember, you have the blood of Jesus as a weapon.

The eyes of this spirit have a glary stare because they are covered with scales (pride) and lack eyelids. God gave men eyelids to protect their natural vision and to keep "foreign" objects out of them. Eyelids clean up the vision. (*Is your vision clean, or is it tainted with greed or other fleshly poisons?*) This snake spirit has scales over its eyes and always has a blurry vision. No plan is ever completely clear. (Visions should be written and made plain for every one to see and run with it). It uses men to cover up by manipulating the saints of God. It is a scheming spirit. We should believe God, not try to scheme Him. The tainted vision of this spirit is deceptive, self-seeking, unproductive and impoverished. This spirit is closely associated with the spirit of Jezebel, the spirit of Belial and the spirit of Behemoth. All three are strongholds and like to rule over territories. The Behemoth spirit likes to rule over nations (this is a crocodile spirit which is in the snake family).

In the mouth of a rattlesnake, are two teeth called fangs that point backwards. The teeth are not there to chew their prey, but to put them in a "hold" so that the snake can swallow them in one piece. The spirit of Leviathan holds you as prey. The tongue of this spirit is split. On one side truth is spoken (that's what holds you in). On the other side is a lie. As a result, it produces deception. Once you are in the mouth of this spirit, it swallows you whole. By the time you realize what's happening, the damage is already done. You are wounded, rejected, betrayed and full of hurt. Had it not been for *the nest*, I would not have had the strength to deal with the spirit of Leviathan.

While riding into the city of Pottstown, I recently saw the face of a skeleton that was missing the lower part of his jawbone. In the forehead the word "Zero" was written. In my spirit I felt that the Lord was telling me, "Leviathan's jawbone is broken and his fangs are missing. His bite is worth nothing". The devil has no hold on you! Because of the blood of Jesus, he has been exposed, enclosed and disposed. I thank God for *the nest*.

GET READY, GET SET, DON'T GO UNTIL YOU ARE SENT

Make sure that you are ready for ministry before you take that step up to the plate. Let *the nest* train you for the reign. Seminary, bible college and ministry license means nothing to demons. They only mean something to man. I am not against going to ministry schools. I have attended one myself. However, you need to understand that there is a school of the spirit that teaches a wealth of wisdom. In this school you learn to apply the knowledge of God's Word to your life through trials and tribulations. Demons respond to the authority that the believer possesses in the Word of God, the blood of Jesus and the name of Jesus. When you apply the Word of God to your own life, it is much easier to walk in your God given authority. Let the Word of God that is in your head, work its way to your heart. Anybody can get licensed. Anybody can go. *Don't go until you are sent.* Learn to overcome your own personal battles and then you can help others overcome theirs. The power for ministry is hidden within your own personal victories.

In *the nest*, God deals with your *"individual self"*, cleans up your *"individual mess"* and develops your *"individual character"*. It is time that you find true shelter in the mess of your nest. By the way, I found out that most of the mess in my nest was my own. How can you help others if you can't help yourself? God will test all that he has placed in you. When the enemy decides to spit in your face, you're going to need what *the nest* has to give. Again, I thank God for *"the nest"*.

STORM RIDER

Although I arrived in flight as a worshipping warrior, "*My freedom was still under fire*" (that is the freedom to worship God in *spirit* and in *truth*). The devil is after your worship. True worshippers have eagle spirits. They soar high to get in the face of God to spot their prey. They pray as they seek their prey. They don't struggle. They go with the flow! The destiny of any eagle is to soar above storms. There is no need for an eagle (a true worshipper) to flap his flesh, when he can soar on the winds of the spirit and get the job done quickly and effectively. As they soar, they spot their prey from the air. It is much easier to expose a demon from the air when you go up in worship.

I have learned how to ride storms until they land me in the designated places set up by God Himself. To ride a storm is to worship God through the problem, no matter what pain, rejection or hurt that is involved. You worship God for who He is. He never stops His "duty as God" when your problems show up. Your true worship is connected to your true trust and faith in God's sovereignty. You love Him when you are up and when you are down. I have learned the *power of true worship*. I am sure there are more storms and I am certain there are more rides. I don't run from storms now, I look for them. *This is my life as an eagle.*

I'M A STORM RIDER

 217

FREEDOM UNDER FIRE

I arrived in flight with wings of strength,
With orders from God, cause I'd been sent.
The forces of hell bombarded the plan,
with fear that I would take a stand.
I held my peace and soared even higher,
As the Holy Ghost told me,
"YOUR FREEDOM'S UNDER FIRE!"

I've got your back, and I'll stand for your cause,
I'll speak My Word, and cause them to PAUSE.
Don't you move, stay right in the flight,
I AM the wind, that give your wings might.

I saw some shells that I'd left in the nest,
Again I remembered to walk in HIS rest.
For it was not real, but a game with my mind,
an illusion of the shells that I had left behind.
I held my peace, and soared a little higher,
Now Jesus said,
"YOUR FREEDOM'S UNDER FIRE!"

When Jesus spoke, every knee had to bow
To the King of kings, and the Lord of the hour.
I arrived in flight, with "A voice to be heard".
My enemies speak, *not even a word.*
Watch out o' bird, you king of the air.
Soar as the eagles, 'cause this freedom
is rare!!!

(Stay Free, Be Key, Set the Captives Free)

My Sister! My Brother!

My sister!   My brother!   Wherever you are
I prayed for your life cause you're on my heart

I feel all your pain and see all the shame
I want you to know that God knows your name

He showed me in prayer as I lay on my face
Your burdensome heart as I stood in your place

Though the sin had you bound and out of your mind
God has your card, and it's in His time

I lay there in tears as I called out your name
I felt the yoke break "In Jesus Name"

When it lifted off of me, I knew that it was well
I knew that your soul would not burn in hell.

I trust my Lord when, He speaks to me a word
You shall be saved, I know this I heard.

ACKNOWLEDGEMENTS

I HONOR you *"My Husband"* for giving me the moral, financial, emotional support, and encouragement to walk in the anointing that the Lord has placed on my life. You are a great provider and a Man of Wisdom. Thanks for your understanding during the many hours that I spent on this assignment. God couldn't have given me a better person to bring out the best in me. You would not let me quit. You are a ram in the bush. I LOVE YOU!

To my own Bobby, Simone, Victoria, Victor Jr. and god-daughter Sade : May the seeds of this fruit land on your ground. These words shall nurture you, in days to come. No matter what happens in your life, remember that you can overcome any obstacle set in your way. Bind the word of the Lord on your hand for a sign, and they shall be as frontlets between your eyes. Battles are sure to come, fight the good fight of faith. You are a winner. Possess your land. If you stray, I declare that you won't stay away. May the Lord prosper you first, Spirit, soul and body. Take this torch and run with it. Love the Lord your God with all your heart, soul and might. Run this race with patience and fear not. There's much ahead for you. Just as Jesus has already prayed for you, so have I.

Mommy

Be Strong in the Lord. Don't leave the nest before your God appointed time. You are sealed in his blood.

I Will Always Love You!

To any and everyone in my biological family. God separated me for years to break, make and shape me. He did it just for you. *Repair The Breech and Return To Your Maker. Reconnect with the God of your salvation-****JESUS CHRIST****.* I love you with the love of the Lord. I give many thanks to God for my *Grandma whom I loved so dearly. She* passed the torch to me months before she died. I will never forget all that she poured into me at the family reunion. She charged me for the call. She never called herself a preacher or a prophet, but that is all she was. Tradition had her veiled within the Body of Christ, though now she sees as He sees. I will not allow the traditions of men and the spiritual terrorism of their opinions of women, cause me to cover my head and draw back from the call. I am undercover but not covered up. *I will carry on the work. I thank God for the mantle.*

To my biological father, I've always wanted you to know the real me, up under all the smiles and jokes. You are so much fun to be around. I can't change the past but I can affect my future with you. Thanks for helping me when I was going through a divorce. You touched the little girl in me. This is for you daddy.   *I LOVE YOU!*

To my biological mother, I thank you for doing the best that you could to raise me. May the joy of the Lord be your strength and I pray that this will clear up your every wound and hurt and give you much understanding about the war within. Remember, *I LOVE YOU* and the generational curses have been destroyed. Cry no more, because the buck stops **HERE. *This book is for you! Receive it as your portion.***

Sis. Kathy Curran, The Word of God came to life in my life when you broke bread and fed me. Thank You for taking me under your wings, you really believed in me. You are a Great teacher and mentor of the Word! This is the fruit of your labor. Thanks for teaching me about the Blood Covenant. You hold a very special place in my heart, I Love You!

Sis. Mary Wrest, You Go Girl, You really Know Your Stuff!
Everything that you taught me about spiritual warfare has paid off. Without your part, this whole walk would have been one of defeat. I've had to walk through all that you taught me. Every ounce of it! You are a stalker of the devil! I will never forget your classes. You had me on the edge of my seat! With Much Love!

Pastors Carl and Anne Scorsone, Thank You! You were the first to allow me to try my wings. You shall reap great benefits. God was and is my healer and you were assistants in the recovery room. Thanks for giving me a chance. *I Love You!*

Rev. Ruth A. Jordan (Heart of Truth Ministries of Norristown, PA), Thank you for your spiritual, physical and professional help in editing this book. Thanks for holding me up until it was done right. You are an awesome woman of God. You said so many things that impacted me, as you corrected these pages. Your expertise helped to bring order to the words written. My deepest thanks to you! God bless you!

To: All of my family in the nest

We wrote it together, we suffered it together, now let's share it together. Thanks for being **IRON** instruments of God in my life. I will never forget you. Thanks for making things happen for me. You will always be a part of my past, present and future. I thank God for the love that we now walk in. We are in a blood covenant for life. God has honored you for your endeavors in His divine kingdom. Your commitment to excellence and ministry is greatly needed. Your entire body mentors many. **Remember, Cut the cord, but don't break the blood.**

God Bless You Port Huron, Michigan!

Let's Soar!   **I LOVE YOU GUYS!**

"Mom and Dad",

Apostle William T. Nichols
Prophetess Vedar Nichols

As far as I am concerned, every person in the Body of Christ needs to come across your path. You are the greatest! My love for you is more than you know. Dad I thank you for releasing mom to minister to women like myself. Without your support, this couldn't have happened. You are a true Apostle and a very merciful man. Thanks for so much mercy when there should have been judgment. Mom, anyone that feeds the birds as you do, they are true Angels. I will always adore you. Your beautiful wings have gone up in the face of many men and women that will never be the same again. The apostolic thrust that you and dad flow in have torn down many demonic strongholds and built up many powerful vessels in the Body of Christ. My life will never be the same since you obeyed the Lord and took me in. I promise to give you the honor that you are due. Keep up the good, God work. You have paid a great price. Your reward shall be great!

All Glory Be Unto Our Lord And Savior Jesus Christ.
Thank you for giving to the Lord, I was a life that was changed.
May the wind of God cause your wings to be strengthened by the
moment, remember Eagles don't fly they SOAR!

**To My Blood Covenant Family
"The True Worshippers"**

The Body of our Lord and Savior Jesus Christ,
"It ain't over until God says it's over".
You shall reign with Christ in all of His glory.
Don't leave your nest before it's time to soar!!!
"We shall be caught up to meet him".

Order Form

Fax orders: 610 792-2640

To order more copies of this book please send correspondence to:

Thorns In My Nest
P.O. Box 1005
Royersford, PA 19468

Name :_____ __
Address:_____
City _____State _____Zip: _____-_____
Telephone:_____
Email address:_____
Number of Copies_____

* * *Send check or money order, No cash please!

Order Form

Fax orders: 610 792-2640

To order more copies of this book please send correspondence to:

𝕿𝖍𝖔𝖗𝖓𝖘 𝕴𝖓 𝕸𝖞 𝕹𝖊𝖘𝖙
P.O. Box 1005
Royersford, PA 19468

Name :_____ __
Address:_____
City _____State _____Zip: _____-_____
Telephone:_____
Email address:_____
Number of Copies_____

***Send check or money order, No cash please!